By the same Author

ONE FINE DAY

OOTACAMUND IN 1837. FROM AN AQUATINT BY CAPTAIN RICHARD BARRON. SHOWING ST. STEPHEN'S CHURCH
(centre) AND SIR WILLIAM RUMBOLD'S HOUSE, LATER THE CLUB (left)

Victoria and Albert Museum

OOTY PRESERVED

A Victorian Hill Station

BY

MOLLIE PANTER-DOWNES

Illustrated

HAMISH HAMILTON
LONDON

First published in Great Britain, 1967
by Hamish Hamilton Ltd
90 Great Russell Street London WC1

Copyright © 1967 by Mollie Panter-Downes

PRINTED IN GREAT BRITAIN
BY EBENEZER BAYLIS AND SON, LTD.
THE TRINITY PRESS, WORCESTER, AND LONDON

TO MISS KATHLEEN MYERS
OF THE NILGIRI LIBRARY
WITH AFFECTION

Illustrations

PART ONE

'WELCOME!' says the big signboard by the side of the road as the car completes the corkscrew ascent from the heat of the South India plains into an almost alarming coolness. 'WELCOME TO OOTACAMUND, QUEEN OF HILL STATIONS!' Digesting this bland piece of information and feeling a trifle light-headed after all the dizzy loops of the mountain pass, I fancy I can hear, borne faintly on the delicious eucalyptus-scented air, a disparaging sniff from Simla, the Queen of the North, who used to be hostess to a Viceroy, forsooth, instead of a mere Governor of Madras, and whose fame is greater and whose views of the snows, it cannot be denied, are more uplifting to the spirit. Can there be two Queens in the sub-continent? For Kipling, I know, Simla wore the crown, with the preposterous Mrs. Hauksbee as her violet-eyed handmaiden, and there were no contenders. Yet this, I feel, is clearly the authentic royal 'we'. It is the stately official greeting from another of the leftover loves of the British in India, who has been signing herself for miles back on all the milestones that have led me to her—as though she were one of the vanished *mem-sahibs* sitting at her bureau scribbling chits to friends saying 'Do come'— by the affectionate pet name 'Ooty', which suits her best. I conclude that the full four syllables would be a tight fit to get in, and anyway, as I have discovered before coming here, everyone uses the Anglicised diminutive.

'So you are going to Ooty. Lovely Ooty!' someone said

fondly not very long ago in a London room where the lights were on, for it was a dark winter afternoon. 'Nice place, Ooty,' says the driver who has brought me up from the steamy heat and coconut-palm forests of his native Kerala. The Cockneyfied improvization has always stuck to her, though one Governor of Madras in the eighteen-fifties did, in an access of mistaken loyalty, unsuccessfully try to canvass support for the notion that she should be rechristened Victoria. After Independence in 1947, no nationalist fervour swept the diminutive away, decreeing that in future the place would keep to her full Indian name —a beautiful one, to be sure, but a mystery when it comes to deciding its etymological ancestry. Whotakaymund, Wootacamund, Wuttasamund, Ottakalmandu—many versions exist of what it was called long ago, when no one was here but the aboriginal tribe, the Todas, sitting on the green hills with their herds of buffaloes like a pastoral people in the Old Testament, as they still sit today, though (like the British in Ooty) in greatly depleted numbers. And what does the name mean? Is it a mixture of debased Toda words? Or is it, as I have read, a sort of sandwich of Toda and Tamil, the principal language of the South—the Tamil *whotai*, for a species of dwarf bamboo that grows in the forests, and *kai*, meaning fruit or green stuff, in the middle, with the Toda *mund*, a village, clapped on at the end? The scholars disagree, but at some unrecorded moment during the last hundred and forty-six years, a loud, calm English voice pronounced for Ooty, which suits everybody.

Now that I am here, I find myself inevitably echoing the astonishment of all the early visitors who struggled up to Ootacamund, seven thousand three hundred and seventy-eight feet above sea level in the Nilgiri Range—the celebrated Blue Hills of South India, which rise to nearly nine thousand feet out of the scorching tableland of the states of Mysore and Madras. The hills must have seemed an impossible barrier of mountain and jungle in those days to anybody who wondered what lay hidden away among their curiously shaped crags. Today, of course, getting here is easy; in a way, the speed of the journey only increases the surprise of arrival. The traveller from Madras goes on the wings of an Indian Airways Fokker Friendship plane, which drones steadily, hardly appearing to move in the still air, across the fantastic tawny land to Coimbatore, an up-and-coming industrial town fifty-four miles—nearly all of them vertical—from Ooty. From there, you can motor the short distance to Mettupalayam and take the slow, puffing little train, with its engine at the rear, which shoves the few carriages up into the hills, with long pauses for panting and reflection. Or you can hire an ancient taxi and sit, first sweating, then gratefully cooling off, on its bony back seat, while the road zigzags higher and higher, among damp, mossy smells and frequent noticeboards warning of the lethal effects of passing on the hair-raising bends. Or you can come, as I have done, by road all the way from Calicut, on the coast of Kerala, via Mysore, with the jungle dropping away from the sheer edge of the road—silent and hot, full of sleeping game that wakes up at twilight and (my driver informs me) can often be seen crossing the road, a flash of stripes or a dappled streak bounding off in the motorist's headlights.

As the car climbs, the air begins to freshen. The tilted landscape straightens out and rolls away gently on either side in grassy rounded hills that remind me of the Sussex Downs at home. The queenly noticeboard, standing like a hostess at the top of a staircase, welcomes us graciously. We have arrived. Peering out of the car, I see terracotta buildings, Victorian gables, and a house with whimsical turrets that might be in Wimbledon. A fox terrier goes by, attached to an elderly European man, and I reach for a woolly. 'Nice place, Ooty, but too cold,' adds my driver tolerantly, when he drops me at my hotel. He, too, produces an enormous muffler and winds it around his neck; with a Thermos flask of some warming beverage

5

sticking out of a bag beside him, he looks all equipped for a football game.

The British who toiled up through the dense malarial jungle to Ootacamund in the nineteenth century must have found the journey no joke. If you were young and vigorous, you rode. If you were older, or young and lazy, you could go by bullock cart or be carried in a palanquin. According to an early guidebook to the Nilgiris (or Neilgherries, in the original spelling), the bullock carts averaged four and a half to five miles an hour; the horses did five to six, but they tired more quickly. The bullock-cart traveller's luggage was put in the wagon, boards were laid across the valises, and his bedding was placed on the top. Reclining regally thereon, he was towed away, with stops for refreshment and rest at the dak bungalows. Or he could refresh himself, having taken the precaution of seeing to it, as the guidebook strongly recommends, that the sides of the bullock cart were fitted with pockets of coarse cloth into which could be stowed the wine, the beer, the brandy, the kettle, the sacred teapot, and the other vital necessities of Indian life. By whatever means the visitors came, they were soon in ecstasies of amazement and delight. The newly discovered Ootacamund was hailed with rapture as a miraculous giver of health, even of life itself. In the Madras Presidency, where the temperature often stood at 110° or more for months on end, disease, death, and rapid burial were grim commonplaces of daily existence. A youthful subaltern called Walter Campbell—a spirited boy of seventeen, fresh from the Highlands, who kept a careful journal of his experiences—describes the gloom that descended on his regiment when, in 1830, it received orders to embark for India: 'This news fell like a thunderbolt on many. India was to them a land of hopeless banishment—a living grave—a blank in their existence—a land from whence, if they escaped an early death, they were to return with sallow cheeks, peevish tempers, and shattered constitutions. And such, alas, was the fate of many.' Three years later, riding, unshattered and lively still, up to Ootacamund on leave, he gets his first glimpses of the marvellously soft green hills, and he records his awestruck feelings: 'It was like passing through the Valley of Death to Paradise!'

So it must have seemed indeed. Could this possibly be India? In their letters and journals, the Victorian soldiers and administrators and travellers who made the laborious ascent searched their memories for some place at home with which to compare these endless gentle hills, beginning then to be dotted with red-tiled English bungalows surrounded by English flowers that quickly got their toes down into the sub-continent and rampaged like runner beans. Dr. John James, Bishop of Calcutta, writing to the Governor of Madras, the Right Honourable Stephen Lushington, in 1830, declared that 'Malvern at the *fairest* season' was the nearest he could recall. Thomas Babington Macaulay, after a less fortunate stay in June, 1834, when he was holed up with his books here by deluging monsoon rain that prevented him from setting foot outside, wrote feelingly that Ooty had 'very much the look of a rising English watering-place'. Never a great student of nature, he told his sister in England that the scenery on the way up the wild and savage pass had put him domestically in mind of 'the vegetation of Windsor Forest or Blenheim spread over the mountains of Cumberland'. It was a compliment; India had surprised him by imitating the royal hunting reserve, the nobleman's park. A notably disenchanted visitor, Edward Lear, arriving exactly forty years later, looked around and thought glumly of Leatherhead. 'Imagine,' Lord Lytton, Viceroy of India from 1876 to 1880, wrote ecstatically to his wife while staying at Government House in this 'paradise'—as he, too, called it—'imagine Hertfordshire lanes, Devonshire downs, Westmorland lakes, Scotch trout streams . . .' The fact that, like Macaulay, he had struck the rainy season in Ootacamund made no difference, but rather the reverse.

7

'Such beautiful *English* rain, such delicious *English* mud,' his happy pen spluttered along.

It was not India; it was the little patch of England that each exile discovered it to be. Or, rather, it was an English dream made a shade delirious and out of the true by the thin, high air, combined with all that many a heart loved with passion in India—the outdoor life, the horses, the wild animals, the early wakings in the Indian mornings, with their matchless dazzling purity that makes each day seem the first ever created. The lanes, the downs, the tumbling streams were all there, to be tamed and enjoyed as much as possible in the likeness of home. The climate had a touch of savagery about it, true, that did not fit in altogether with any homesick recollection of the mountains of Cumberland or of Malvern, even at its fairest. Ooty is eleven degrees north of the equator, and far south of the Sahara desert. On two hundred and thirty-eight mornings of the year, according to the computations of my old guidebook, the sun rises high and bright and scorching in the heavens and flays the skin off a newcomer unwary enough to go out bareheaded for a long walk in its dangerous early rays. The equatorial sunshine has not been tamed, as one is misled into thinking it has, into an imitation of a perfect June day in England. Under the warmth, the air has a nip of ice. It is an atmospheric *bombe surprise*, in which you sample layers of heat and cold by stepping out of the sun into the shade of the trees, where you shiver immediately and need a sweater. In January and February, the ice can be real. The nights are so sharp that before dawn the roses and Canterbury bells and fat mauve stocks in Ooty gardens may be tipped with frost. There are blankets on your bed, and a hot-water bottle between the sheets. To the early British visitors, that alone was worth every step, every jolt and aching muscle of the long, arduous journey. 'A chilblain!' yipped a Victorian lady, proudly exhibiting her reddened finger. Oh, the joys of a tingling blue nose, a hot grog! Could this be India? Then, as now,

8

there was inordinate satisfaction in the climate—'the best in the world', you will hear it often and complacently described today by the remaining European residents—and there seems some sort of tacit implication that the British, when they created Ootacamund, may have ordered up the weather from some Elysian cold storage in Madras, along with the engineers to build the roads, and the teak and the carpenters and the labourers for the houses of the budding community.

'Where could you get better?' a smiling Indian lady, whose weather it now indubitably is, challenges me soon after I arrive in Ooty, and it is hard to answer. Has it not been compared to an autumn in the South of France—as golden, but without the mistral—and to a North Persian spring? But I suspect that only the well-to-do really enjoy the colder months here, and that my driver spoke for the general run of townsfolk who have drifted up to Ooty from other parts of India. You see bundles of shawls wrapped into a complete cocoon, except for an eye looking through a chink and thin legs protruding at the bottom, gathered around the glaring lamp of a rickety teahouse on a nipping January night; the old people, especially, look cruelly pinched. One of the recurring figures in the Ootacamund landscape of green grass, terraced red earth, and giant eucalyptus trees is that of an old woman in a shabby sari quietly, carefully, eternally picking up sticks. There is hardly a tree that does not display its cicatrices where limbs have been lopped in the constant battle of the poor to keep warm. Nameboards outside houses sometimes disappear overnight, and signposts have been known to vanish, too. One night soon after I arrived at my hotel—a rambling Victorian structure perched on a shady platform of ground above distant voices calling and arguing, cows lowing, drums tapping, and radio music mournfully screeching in the town below the hill—a whole tree was cut down silently in the garden and nimbly carted away before dawn by persons unknown (though the hotel's redoubtable Scottish proprietress said darkly that she had a very good notion of the culprits' identities). Even the wealthy Indians who own houses in Ooty mostly prefer to come up in April and May, when the place is at its loveliest and when 'everyone' in the Nilgiris—and people from far beyond, too—turns out for the races and goes to the celebrated Ooty Flower Show and to the hotly contested dog show, and the maharajahs who still have imposing 'palaces' here are in residence, and the hotels are packed, and the club is full, and the normally quiet roads hum with cars. 'It is a pity you cannot be here for it,' a British acquaintance commiserates with me, a winter visitor. 'Then you would be seeing Ooty more as it used to be. For two months of the year, anyway, it is itself.'

I wonder what it is, then, that I am seeing, for there never was a place that seemed more fully in possession of a self, or so strongly a quintessence of a vanished epoch, and if one has to people it largely with ghosts nowadays, that in no way alters one's sense that it has remained remarkably well preserved, as though embalmed under the glass of this rarefied air that makes one's heart bump and diminishes one's enthusiasm for walking up even the smallest hill for the first week or two. Embalming suggests death, but before you have had time to take more than a quick look round, someone is sure to tell you (with a resigned sigh if your informant is a member of the old European community, anxious about the damage that changes may inflict on the natural beauty of the hill station) that Ooty is far from moribund. Fresh revenue, employment, and life, you will be informed, are about to be siphoned into a place that for a hundred and forty years or so drew all three mainly from its existence as a suspended playground to which the British came in large numbers to visit and to live. Though Ooty's past is over, modern India, full of enthusiasm and energy and know-how, is coming to rescue the old girl.

Just at first, though, I am disinclined to look ahead at

10

the future, being as astonished by everything as was the early lady visitor with the chilblain. I am (perhaps because of the altitude) in shape to take in only crumbs of easy, nourishing information, such as are usefully served up on yet another large noticeboard, this one opposite the handsome Anglican church of St. Stephen's, built in 1830, which sits as firmly as a nested hen on a wooded little hill above where several roads meet and a smart policeman, wearing a dashingly folded puggaree, stands on his own small eminence, waving the buses, the bullock carts, the bicycles, and the cars on their way. The board tells me, among sundry details about public parks and municipal latrines and the local literacy rate (a high one, of over fifty per cent), that Ooty has a population of fifty thousand-odd. 'It used to be a dear little village when I first came to live here,' one of the European residents laments to me, 'and now it's suddenly become a town.' What principally surprises me is that so much of the village unmistakably survives. I am content for several afternoons to moon around the lanes that reminded Lord Lytton of Hertfordshire, and to gaze at the names on the gates of the pretty bungalows, which new Indian owners seldom seem to have altered in favour of anything more local. They remain inclining wistfully towards England, being strong, at opposite ends of the feudal salt, on Halls and Cottages. On a large-scale map of Ootacamund I find Apple Cottage, Ethel Cottage, Hopeful Cottage, and triumphant Cheerful Cottage. There are, more grandly, Woodcock Hall and Squire's Hall, to bring a breath of the shires and crisp autumn mornings out with the guns to these back roads where the geraniums in someone's garden are growing as high as an elephant's eye, and a bright, unidentified bird flashes like a sequin out of a hedge of vast, fleshy white bellflowers. Some houses have romantic literary godparents, like Kenilworth and Bleak House. Others are geographically allusive, like Harrow-on-the-Hill and Grasmere Lodge, and a few, in as complicated a vein of whimsical archness as you could hope

11

to find among the seaside shanties in an English coastal colony, have been given coy names like the Castlet and Idyll Hallo Ween. Though many of their owners may be away, the bungalows are trim and their flower beds look well tended. Only here and there do I see a house that has obviously fallen on hard times and is tenanted by several poor families, with a compound where no flowers bloom but where thin dogs wander, and washing flaps on an ancient, bald tennis court, and the roof tiles are smashed to the size of pebbles on a beach, and the radio going full blast mingles with a clatter of shrill voices from within.

Down in the town, one of the principal road junctions, nostalgically named Charing Cross, in no way resembles the original. I go in to buy postcards and a bottle of ink at the bookseller's and stationer's called Higginbotham's—a branch of the big one in Madras—outside which a chalked board announces that the plays of George Bernard Shaw have 'just arrived'. Rejecting a bemused idea that they have just been written, too, I drop in at the Ooty Club, where I have been accepted as a temporary member, for tea and toast, or stroll over to read the *Observer* (two months old, which gives it a piquant new flavour) under the dusty antlered heads that gloom from the walls of the reading room of the Nilgiri Library.

It is in the vicinity of Higginbotham's, or of Spencer's excellent food, drug, and hardware store, where you can buy anything from a tinned Dundee cake to penicillin or a suitcase, and where the strawberry boys squat beside their rush baskets heaped with Ooty berries—coral-coloured, small, and sweet, arranged on fern with as much natural elegance as if they were being displayed by a *maître d'hôtel* on the central table of a smart Paris restaurant—that one's dreamy sense of having been here before comes most perfectly into flower. Here one sees of a morning some of the remaining European ladies, dressed in tweeds and Aertex blouses, shod strongly with brogues, and perhaps topped with a large topee, wending their way with baskets, library books, and the air of building an interim Cheltenham in India's green and not too unpleasant exile. There are, officially, no British in Ooty any longer, one notes. They have become 'Europeans', taking the spiritual cross-Channel trip rather in advance of their government at home in 'U.K.', as they refer invariably to that remote but still benign presence. The authentic English village-shop atmosphere survives in Spencer's. As the clerks flit to and fro, snatches of gossip boom across the aisles. 'You add three-quarters of a pound of sugar to a pint of juice— no need for the full pound, dear, unless you like it very sweet,' someone is saying, patting the neat white waves under her hairnet. 'I always declare that you are one of the two ladies who know everyone in Ooty!' a stout matron cries effusively to a formidable-looking old woman, who receives the remark with a grunt. The ages of the European customers, I note respectfully, have a certain uniformity. I overhear one lady, waiting for the spectacled clerk to complete a grocery order, remark to a friend, 'She's only seventy, you know,' to which the friend replies, 'Yes, I remember her mother.' The baskets fill up meanwhile with Rose's Lime Juice, chocolate biscuits, and toothpaste and marmalade and aspirin that look as like as two pins to the goods that their owners would be putting in them from the shelves of a village store in Somerset. Closer inspection, however, reveals the lettering 'Made in India' somewhere on the labels. This is not Cheltenham, I have to conclude as I leave the shop, skirting the strawberry boys and a basket of bedding plants displayed at the door, near a noticeboard on which I read hand-written advertisements announcing that a litter of adorable retriever pups are for sale to good homes and that somebody heading back to U.K. wishes to dispose of a Singer sewing machine and a station wagon, cheap. If I do not immediately spot a Tudor café at which the ladies will be able to get their morning coffee when they finish here, I feel that one is probably just round the corner—perhaps

13

not far from the charming little Hindu shrine, decorated with brightly painted plaster bulls, that I came across somewhere on yesterday's walk.

It could never be Cheltenham, for the chaste Regency lines and the creamy or sugar-icing stucco are not here, though some of the oldest and most affluent houses, built by nabobs who preferred to retire to Ooty, thinking that they had struck the next thing to an Indian Utopia, have imposing front verandas upheld by stately classic columns. One or two sit on their hillsides (Ooty is spread out over a whole series of small hills) facing the sun in passable colonial imitation of the Greek. But the architectural style of most of Ootacamund's principal buildings is that of the eighteen-sixties or thereabouts, when the place was expanding fast. It recalls the Victorian resort, running to a wealth of sharp gables with elaborately fretted bargeboards and touches of ironwork and spines of decorative *chevaux de frise* bristling along roof-tops to the inconvenience and possible vital injury of strolling cats. The prevailing colour is a deep terra-cotta red, here and there with white stone trim. It is a style that flourishes, too, in quiet residential streets of Putney or Harrow; the difference is that these are Victorian buildings sawed off mostly to one-storey cottage height, and their scale and looks, together with an elusive flavour of the Swiss chalet and the cuckoo clock, put me vaguely in mind of toy railway stations ornamented with cut-out curlicues. But instead of the expected tin porter pushing a luggage barrow, and a shiny passenger or two walking about in front of them, there are gossiping groups of men in shabby puggrees, clasping large umbrellas. Schoolgirls in muslin blouses and with the bright-green or cornflower skirts of their school uniforms down to their ankles rush along laughing, their arms piled up with books and their glossy pigtails streaming; a man sits on his heels behind a little pavement stall of oranges and chopped lengths of sugar-cane; a wandering cow or a bullock cart goes by, the

14

bullock's horns painted blue, or perhaps one of Ootacamund's native tribe of ponies, who roam at will over its
green hillocks and hollows but are saddled up in the
season, I am told, and are greatly in demand for giving
children rides.

The Collector's Office, the very heart of Ooty, where all
manner of permits must be applied for, is a rambling
arcaded building, built in 1866 and rather charming, with
its glassed-in upper verandas and airy arches. In front of
it is a little plot of garden that used, I learn, to offer
passersby the sight of the best lawn turf in Ooty but now
has been patriotically dug up and planted with utilitarian
cauliflowers, as an example to encourage the community
to support India's urgent national campaign to grow more
food. The cauliflowers look very fine, too. It is a sardonic
local joke to say that one morning they will all have disappeared as mysteriously as the nameboards outside
bungalows. Ooty is a poor town. When I approach the
Collector's Office, a rattle of typewriters floats from a door-
way, and, peering up a staircase, I catch a whiff of the odour
of bureaucracy—a Dickensian blend of office paste, ancient
forms tied with musty pink tape and filed in bursting
pigeonholes, and dust—which the British maybe imported
with the weather. I pass through a group of men who are
hanging about the porch, presumably waiting to see the
great man or one of his underlings, and have the air of
being prepared to stick around for days, if need be.
Around the corner, perched on a knoll, is the Post Office,
which faces, across a stony strip of red earth, the Law
Court—another building out of a Victorian nursery set,
with a minuscule clock tower, Time in a sentry box,
pointing a red finger, sharp as a bayonet, sternly against
the bright blue sky. Nothing is happening there at the
moment, but the law, I have been told, is popular in Ooty.
People enjoy litigation and indulge in it frequently, often
against members of their own families. In the Post Office,
my letters plump into the slit marked 'Air Mail', which is

as strictly utilitarian as the cauliflowers, but on my walks through the town I have come across one or two tall, thin, scarlet pillar boxes of venerable aspect, crowned with pagodalike roofs finished off elegantly by knobs shaped something like tiny pineapples, on which the cipher 'V. R.' is surmounted by the royal coat of arms. Like the remaining British in Ootacamund and the enigmatic Todas, these elderly edifices (as you can only, and politely, call them) are survivors and reminders of the past that is on its way out. In time, they will probably be replaced by the more usual tubby, unadorned pillar boxes, which have no elegance and do not receive my letters with the air of old-fashioned rectitude that promises safe passage, even to U.K. and beyond. The royal arms certainly have no meaning today for those bright schoolgirls tossing their plaits and running along to their date with modern India, though there are a number of photographs of Elizabeth Regina in Ooty, hanging on the walls of shops as well as in the club and in the homes of patriotic exiles—with the Duke and without, in diadem and low *décolletage* spanned by the blue ribbon of the Garter, or tricorned and attractively military on her charger at the Trooping of the Colour. (I even caught the eye of a coloured picture of George IV in a grocer's shop the other day. He looked florid, stout, and uneasy, and a long way from the Pavilion in Brighton. I think he was advertising biscuits.) Yet it will be a pity, I feel, if one of these scarlet boxes is not allowed to survive intact as a footnote to a chapter of history—unloved, perhaps, but India's history still.

PART TWO

THE curtain rose on Ootacamund about three hundred and sixty-four years ago, then went down again with a thud. For two hundred years or so, the place disappeared from sight among the towering, formidable Nilgiris, which successfully kept their marvellous secret hidden from the profane eyes of the foreign invaders. On one thing all are agreed, in spite of the arguments that gathered later on as to who was their real discoverer: the Todas were already here when the first European appeared, shivering in the cold mountain air and speaking of a Christian god. If one tries to picture the scene from the description in a contemporary Portuguese manuscript now in the British Museum, it is the seventeenth-century newcomers who appear to be wearing picturesque fancy dress; the Todas look perfectly modern and recognizable, being pretty much as they are today.

Several learned studies have been written about these walking anthropological posers, proving nothing for certain except that they antedated all comers to the Nilgiris by a great, unmeasured parcel of time. Prince Peter of Greece, an anthropologist, wrote a pamphlet, published by the Madras Government Museum in 1951, discussing Sumerian links he had noticed in certain features of the Toda religious ritual, which seemed, he thought, to tie them to the ancient inhabitants of Mesopotamia. Mme Blavatsky was so impressed by their remarkable appearance and supernatural powers that she wrote a book about

19

them. Young men with tape recorders appear now and then to live among them and study their peculiar language, marriage customs, and ceremonies. Film units have recorded them, and tourists' cameras click busily in the *munds* that are in or close to Ooty. It is said that one old Toda long ago was lured by Phineas T. Barnum into his circus for a season. Yet they seem, on the whole, as surprisingly unself-conscious and as resistant to change as they have been durable in the history of Ooty.

I do not see Todas very often in the town. Most of their villages are scattered far out in the hills. Often a village is no more than two or three thatched huts shaped like dog kennels, with no windows or chimney but with a hole in the roof to take the smoke of a fire, and a low entrance at one end, which only Toda babies can manage without going down on all fours, and a circular compound for their buffaloes. The government is beginning to build little modern brick houses to replace the old huts, but they are said to be unpopular. The story one is told is that Todas often put their buffaloes in their new brick houses and prefer to go on living under their tumbledown thatch. They have been here forever, they say, and were created by the gods to be the lords of the Nilgiri soil—a race of pastoralists who must live far away from other men, on the pasture grounds where they graze the herds of large mud-coloured cattle that are their wealth, their life occupation, and the central feature of their complicated and mysterious religion. A river of buffalo milk flows through it like a sacred Ganges. The dairies in which the milk is kept are holy places; the dairymen are its priests. Milking and churning are holy, too, and no woman is allowed to perform either duty. The Todas' principal gods—a brother and sister called On and Tiekirzi—rule the worlds of the dead and the living, respectively, but there are six hundred deities who are Todas themselves and live on the tops of the highest hills, from which they keep a benevolent watch, like immortal herdsmen, over men and buffaloes.

One of the Todas' gods, called Kwoto, once tied down the sun between two mountains for a joke, to show how strong he was, and took it to drink at a stream every day with the herds. When a man dies, some of his beasts are slaughtered at his cremation ceremony, so that he may enjoy their milk and the friendly company of their low, ponderous forms as he journeys (quite literally, the dead are believed to 'go west') towards the Kingdom of On. Todas and buffaloes have been harmoniously involved together for so many uncounted centuries that these deceptively benign-looking creatures, who have mild, wide, intellectual fore-heads like George Eliot's and moist café-au-lait muzzles that invite stroking, seem to sense and immediately take a dislike to outsiders, especially Europeans in their ridiculous garments that have no comfortable, familiar smell of ghee. Sometimes they chase snorting after riders on the downs, and picnic parties settling down to admire the breathtaking views of the Nilgiris as they eat their sand-wiches have been known to take flight until order has been restored by the arrival of a Toda infant nonchalantly flicking a branch.

The tribe's polyandrous habits and the accommodating sexual amorality of its women, which the Christian missionaries and the Hindus in Ooty find shocking, are often cited as the reason for the Todas' sad decline in numbers. For that matter, the outside world's rulings on marriage appear peculiar, if not downright inhuman, to Todas, whose language contains no equivalents for such inflexible civilized words as 'adultery' and 'illegitimate'. No child in a Toda *mund* is ever fatherless; fathers surround a baby in comforting profusion. But a few years ago the tribe had dwindled to about four hundred; better medical care financed by the Government in Delhi has now apparently doubled this figure. Their sterility may be caused by syphilis, and certainly by interbreeding. Women have always been fewer than men, owing to their ancient custom of exposing children of the less useful female sex to be trampled by stampeding buffaloes driven out of the cattle ring. The British Government took a stern line on this in 1856, after which the practice was supposed to have ceased.

People tell you that the Todas will most likely look just like everybody else before long. Already, they say, the children are beginning to wear clothes bought in the bazaar—knickerbockers and woolly coats and magenta hair ribbons—and to be hard to tell from Tamil children. But as yet, to anyone observing them on the roads around Ooty, it is obvious that this is not so, for their appearance is strikingly different. They are much as they were in the attractive old coloured prints of the hill station, which often include a Toda man in the toga-like unstitched garment of coarse homespun cotton, edged with a heavily embroidered red or blue border, that is still worn today, standing on the grassy slopes surveying his buffaloes with his wife, her long corkscrew ringlets shining with a liberal anointing of butter, and one or two babies squatting meekly beside him. As in the world of birds, the female of the species is dingier than the male. Toda men are noticeably taller than the other Ooty dwellers, and many of them are extremely handsome. They have strong features that would look well on a coin, finely shaped heads of long jet-black hair, and curling beards. Both sexes have long, slender hands and feet. The women spend hours massaging their feet with ghee, cutting the nails, and perhaps having them embellished with a little tattooing in a blue Toda snake pattern; a pretty foot with fine, prominent ankle bones is the most admired of feminine charms.

When the Toda men stalk along the country roads twitching their mantles round them, the effect is startlingly patriarchal, and one remembers one of the many ingenious theories propounded by scholars about them— that they may be the Lost Tribe of Israel, to account for a slightly aquiline cast of countenance that might be considered Hebrew. Who are they, and where did they come from before they settled here, out of all India? There is an-

22

GROUP OF TODAS,
1857. FROM AN AQUA-
TINT BY CAPTAIN
RICHARD BARRON
Victoria and Albert Museum

OOTACAMUND, 1891. ST. STEPHEN'S CHURCH (left)

for one day only—October 24th—climbed a hill ('a long and fatiguing walk'), drank and methodically noted the fine, clear water of a spring, and departed. The beauties and possibilities of the place clearly did not strike him, as he sat winded on his hilltop making his calculations and writing up the notes for his report. He gets his breath back, collects his gear, and disappears abstractedly into oblivion.

Two surveyors, a Mr. Keys and a Mr. Macmahon, came to map out the wild Nilgiris in 1812. They seem to have recorded no observations of the trip. The two Englishmen who showed up six years later were very different, one may guess. They were high-spirited young men—a Mr. Whish and a Mr. Kindersley—who were assistants to Mr. John Sullivan, the Collector of Coimbatore. No pictures of them have survived, but they loved shooting and riding, and were fascinated by India—prototypes of the happy extroverts who were later to find their paradise in Ooty. One can imagine them lolling in the evenings under a punkah in Coimbatore, smoking and cooling off after the long, sweltering day, as they gazed thoughtfully at the hazy blue outline of the Nilgiris crouching against the sky—gallery after gallery of hills rising sheer out of a forbidding belt of jungle from five to twenty miles deep. They were planning to take a trip up there when they got the chance, and soon one came along conveniently in the line of duty. The two assistants were sent to round up a gang of tobacco smugglers; when the gang made off into the mountains, the Englishmen set out after them. They were perhaps new to their job and the country. Eventually, they caught up with one of the smugglers, who was hiding in a hut. They were hot and thirsty. Their prisoner offered to fetch some milk from a nearby village, stepped out on the errand, and sensibly melted away into the forest. Whish and Kindersley, nothing daunted, decided to press on, less in the interests of the British Raj, no doubt, than in their curiosity to explore further into the hills. Some Badagas, men of the largest of the Nilgiri hill tribes, had turned up, and they were persuaded to go along as guides to show them the tracks through the jungle. The party set out.

When the young men returned to Coimbatore, where Mr. Sullivan was perhaps not in the best of moods over their absence, they were full of excitement and remarkable stories. After an arduous climb, they said, they had come out into a wonderfully fertile region, about fifty miles across from east to west and eight thousand feet or so, they judged, above sea level. It was a plateau, free of jungle, and they were told that where it had been cultivated (by the Bergers, or Burghers, an agricultural tribe greatly in awe of the mysterious Todas, to whom, as the original men in possession, they paid some sort of tribute), the rich soil produced two crops in a season. Whish and Kindersley had been astounded by the cold at night, which 'turned water into glass', as one of the Badagas described it. Yet by day the hot sun shone brilliantly on views that reminded them of home. Could it really be India? Every thicket in this sportsman's heaven teemed with game. Delighted with their expedition, bursting with enthusiastic descriptions of the extraordinary hidden territory, they poured their stories out to Mr. Sullivan, the Collector. Later, they published an account in a Madras journal, which seems to have aroused little or no interest. No doubt people felt that it was too fantastic to be believed.

Mr. Sullivan, however, had listened with great attention, and he resolved to make an expedition up into the hills to see for himself as soon as he could. John Sullivan is the most important figure in the history of Ootacamund, and is regarded piously by all as the Father of Ooty. Later on, there were those who held that he had not actually been its discoverer, since Whish and Kindersley got there before him, but he was certainly its energetic entrepreneur and devoted lover. A picture of him hangs in the Ootacamund Club, and I see a man with a bland, smooth oval face balanced like an egg in the cup of a high stock. Though not

26

as expansively constructed as was Mr. Jos Sedley, Collector of Boggley Wollah, the body in the frock coat and sponge-bag trousers (no concession to India in the attire) gives an impression of well-nourished Victorian solidity. Mr. Sullivan has been 'taken' sitting in an armchair with his hand resting lightly on a pile of books on a table, while behind him, veiled in gauzy mists, appears to float a vague suggestion of his beloved Nilgiris. His large eyes stare placidly into mine, but something obstinate and a shade querulous seems to have settled like sediment in the line of the compressed lips, and I conclude that, in spite of the blandness, Mr. Sullivan might be a difficult man to cross. He looks, at the time of this picture, about fifty years of age. He may be younger. The egg is enigmatical. Nobody in Ooty is able to tell me how old he was when he became the first European settler, or where he came from in England, or where he retired when he finally left India, for, much as he loved the place, he did not die here.

It was the next year, 1819, before the Collector was able to follow up his assistants' stories. He set out, at last, for a twenty-day tour, taking with him two companions—a distinguished visiting Frenchman, M. Leschenault de la Tour, the Naturalist to the King of France, and an Assistant-Surgeon named Jones. Poor M. Leschenault de la Tour had been brought 'aux portes du tombeau', as he pathetically wrote, by fever, and he must have joined the by no means easy expedition feeling apprehensive over whether his health would be equal to it. Possibly Jones was asked to come along to keep an eye on him. Yet when the party had completed the most difficult and dangerous part of the journey, struggling up from the dark jungle, with its lurking malaria and wild beasts, and coming out on the glorious plateau that Whish and Kindersley had described, the Frenchman forgot his weakened condition in the general excitement. His health improved miraculously. India had brought him almost to the tomb; India

27

now restored him. After they had been in camp two days, he felt completely recovered—able to walk seven or eight miles a day and to take a keen professional interest in the expeditions he made with the others. One likes to think of M. Leschenault de la Tour, armed with his tin box, buzzing happily from flower to flower. And when they returned from the hills, he, too, seized his pen and dashed off to a Madras literary journal a glowing scientific account of the finds he had brought back. '*La collection des plantes que mon ami et moi avons récueillées sur les montagnes de Nilgiris renferme plus de deux cents espèces, parmi lesquelles un grand nombre de nouvelles. . . .*'

The find that Mr. Sullivan brought back was destined to last longer than any of M. Leschenault de la Tour's carefully labelled specimens. His walks and rides in the nervous, buoyant air that had electrified his ailing guest, his views of the rolling green hills, so cool and fresh after the burnt-up plain, had been the start of one of those passionate love affairs with a place that sometimes change the life of a man or woman. He looked thoughtfully at everything and made his plans. He was back again in 1820, this time bringing Mrs. Sullivan with him; by then he had offered the Government in Madras his opinion that a superb health-giving retreat for the British in South India, military and civilian, could be built in the cool climate of the Nilgiris. The Government listened favourable and began the construction of a pass into the mountains in 1821. At the suggestion of the Collector, prisoners from the Coimbatore jail were set to work on the road; in this wilderness, he pointed out, escape was improbable. Mr. Sullivan had already started the building of his own small stone bungalow there. It was finished in 1823, and the first baptism recorded in Ooty was that of his son in May of the same year. From that date, the Collector's wife and children appear to have lived up here permanently, and Coimbatore, as Madras became disapprovingly aware, saw him less and less. He was hooked to Ooty. Mr. Whish and Mr.

Kindersley were possibly left down below, doing all the work of the district, or perhaps by then they had been transferred to another station. They disappear from the picture.

Ootacamund, the Queen of Hill Stations, was still far away, but she was beginning to get started on her career; soon several other British officials took to hankering for a little place of their own in the Nilgiris. To get out into the country has always been a deep-seated instinct of the English townsman. Now to get out of India and into the 'English' climate of this newly discovered health resort sounded too good to be true. Building land was acquired easily enough from the Todas, its rightful owners, for a small compensation of about a rupee an acre. At first, private individuals were the purchasers; in 1828, the Government began more ambitious plans for building a sanatorium for military invalids. The land prices did not long satisfy the Toda tribesmen, who could observe from their pasture slopes the bullock carts plodding up from the plains and the first few cottages beginning to take shape on their lonely hills. 'These people were simple and unacquainted with the value of money,' says a rueful note passing between the Military Commandant of Ooty and the Government in Madras in 1833. 'Now they have become fully aware of its value and try to drive a good bargain.'

But in the early days of innocence Mr. Sullivan was in sole control of Ootacamund. He was the virtual king of the castle, a pioneering Robinson Crusoe who had landed on this extraordinary island site floating above the scorching plains, and he used the opportunity very profitably for his own interests, as was later accusingly brought up against him by the powers in Madras. Those large, calm eyes looked into the future and saw Ooty. By 1829, he held five times as much land as all the other European settlers put together, and it included some of the finest plots. On these he later built houses that he sold or let to

29

the Government for, it was said, very steep prices, which explains the venomous dislike of him that is cantankerously apparent in some of the torrent of memorandums that poured between Ooty or Coimbatore and Madras. One of his most resented feats was to enclose two hundred acres of excellent land on which he said he was going to make agricultural experiments—only somehow the experiments did not come off. He was genuinely interested in agriculture, however. He started plantations of flax and hemp and he imported barley, which was called 'Sullivan *gângi*' even in this century by the tribesmen around Ooty. Hops were tried, but they were one of the few crops that did not take to the Nilgiris.

As for gardening, it was a passion with Mr. Sullivan. He sent for a gardener from England, a Mr. Johnson, who was left in charge of building operations when the Collector had to tear himself reluctantly away to attend to the affairs of his district. With Johnson, in 1821, arrived the first English apple and peach trees and strawberries, the first seeds of flowers and vegetables. How could Mr. Sullivan possibly absent himself in Coimbatore when the raspberries were ripening and the new hollyhocks and the mignonette were about to come out? Potatoes, which are cultivated in a big way today on endless steep terraces carved out of the red hillsides, were introduced by Mr. Sullivan, and they flourished superbly. Practically everything flourished and bloomed prodigiously up here, including the complexions of drooping wives and 'the fresh and chubby juveniles' who were noted many years later by a young lieutenant named Richard Burton—the future great Arabian and African traveller and scholar—who came to Ooty on sick leave in 1847 and admitted, although he disliked the place, that these rosy children were indeed 'quite a different creation from the pallid, puny, meagre, sickly, irritable little wretches who do nothing but cry and perspire in the plains'. Vegetables grew chubby, too, in the marvellously fertile soil. A few years after Mr. Sullivan's arrival, gargantuan

30

(and inedible) wonders were being compared as proudly as though their owners were competing in a village show at home. A beet is recorded as being nearly three feet round, a radish three feet long, and a cabbage plant eight feet high. Geraniums grew in hedges, and somebody's verbena forgot its place and shot up to the sky on a trunk like that of a robust tree. English oaks and firs were planted, to complete the curious illusion of England-in-India, including one specimen, later known as Sullivan's Oak, in the garden of the Collector's cottage, Stonehouse. The fever took hold of everyone. An optimistic gentleman ordered from England a hundred guineas' worth of plants, of which only one dogged currant bush and one hardy pear tree were found to be alive after the long voyage and the slow hoist by bullock cart up from the plains. Yet in 1829 there were wild white strawberries, white Ayrshire roses, and small, deep damask roses growing in Ooty, to give homesick thoughts to the sallow military men and civilians who were beginning to bring their families up to the newly discovered Nilgiris. The Scottish flowers were delightedly noted by a convalescent young officer of the 8th Native Infantry named Samuel Macpherson, who later became well known as the Political Agent in Gwalior at the time of the Mutiny. Writing to his father, a professor of Greek at Aberdeen University, he talks of these hills as 'presenting to the eye a wildered paradise', and so they must have done in the earliest days of all.

In 1830, a Military Commandant was appointed to run the settlement, and to Mr. Sullivan this was the equivalent, it is clear, of the angel with the fiery sword ejecting him from his private Eden. Mr. Sullivan made many strenuous objections to the new Commandant and his innovations, all of which were frowned upon and coldly rejected by the Government in Madras. Actually, matters had been taken out of Mr. Sullivan's control long before this, for Ooty was growing fast, as the ever multiplying communications between the Government, the Collector's Office, and the

31

military showed. The official reports on the Nilgiris over those years are a microcosm of British India. Requests flowed down to Madras without cease for things great and small—for twenty bullockloads of rice; for spare bullocks; for a very urgent order of 'Turbands and Cummerbands'; for money orders for Mrs. E. Warren, widow of a Sergeant W. Warren, of Her Majesty's 89th Regiment, who has just died; for more coolies to make the roads and more carpenters to work on a military hospital; for a special 'hill allowance' to be given to the native troops, as prices are high up here and the climate and altitude of the place are not at all agreeable to them. The opening of a new bazaar, the Commandant dashes off imperatively, is an absolutely top priority; 'otherwise no black man will remain on the hills for lack of provisions'. First stomachs, now legs are the worry. 'The Commanding Officer recommends to the Quartermaster General that cloth trousers be sent up for the use of Pioneers on the hills.' Like Father Ferreiri's porters, the shivering Indian troops are miserable. Requests, ever more requests: for '4 or 5 elephants' to shift trees on the new pass down to Mettupalayam; for wheelbarrows and gunpowder and seasoned teak and engineers and miners; for a pension for the family of the Pioneer Sepoy who was killed by a tiger in the jungle. Men had arrived in the wildered paradise, and they had brought their weaknesses with them: 'The Military Commander points out that the arrack shop is being too heavily patronized by many inhabitants of Ooty.' No answer recorded. Then, Staff Sergeant Baker, who is always drunken and hard-up, and picks quarrels, should be relieved. Two officers, much intoxicated, beat up the bazaar yesterday evening and grievously broke the heads of several respected Hindus. Captain Armstrong does not behave obediently to the Commanding Officer when the C.O. is not in uniform. ('Very bad example to other young men.') And a contractor is alleged to be corrupt, and the butler of the late Captain Leighton must be put on trial for stealing some gold mohurs out of the late Captain's trunk. Even in the health-giving hills, death and illness are a constant refrain. Tigers leap out of the jungle, fever strikes the men, wives die in childbed, and their infants fade. More medical officers are requested. The pens scratch away, and the tempers explode: 'The Military Commandant deprecates the discourteous language used by the Collector.'

It was eleven years since Mr. Sullivan had cast his meditative eye over the lovely, lonely landscape while M. Leschenault de la Tour leaped renewed, a botanical Lazarus, up and down the slopes with his tin box, and sometimes the early days when he and Mrs. Sullivan and their babies camped out in their rough stone cottage, alone in their Nilgiri morning, must have seemed far off and desirable. Now it was a rising place, beset with the usual housing difficulties. The Governor of Madras—then the Right Honourable Stephen Lushington, who started the building of St. Stephen's Church—came up frequently and stayed at the elegant pillared mansion that had been built on a Toda site by a wealthy businessman from Hyderabad, Sir William Rumbold, and that much later became the present Ootacamund Club. It was not until 1869 that the idea of a regular move here in the hot weather of the Governor and the whole secretariat was mooted. Already, however, 'sundry second-chop mandarins and bigwigs of inferior caste', as a contemporary commentator scornfully described them, tried to flock up to the Nilgiris in the wake of Mr. Lushington and his staff. The cheerful English cottages, built of burnt brick and mud or of local stone, were slowly increasing, but there was a timber shortage. The trees had been recklessly felled by the first arrivals for building and for fires. Now, to replace the losses, it was decided to make large plantings of Australian wattle and eucalyptus, which had been brought back as seeds from Tasmania by botanically-minded officers of the old Madras Army. Many people consider that they took to Ooty only

33

too well, for houses and views were swallowed up whole-sale in their luxuriant dark shade.

The Collector appears to have been exceedingly busy with these plantings, and with building his houses and letting them to eager newcomers. Perhaps he was remiss elsewhere—he certainly must have been in his district—and altogether too diligent in planning improvements to the charming little lake that he had had constructed soon after he got here. It had originally been designed for irrigation purposes, but it looked so delightful that it ended up as a piece of purely ornamental water—the Collector's toy and his special pride. The lake was mentioned cruelly in a really shattering dressing down that Mr. Sullivan received about this time from the powers in Madras. What attracted the thunderbolt is not very clear; there may have been many warning rumbles. He appears to have written a pompous public letter rebutting criticisms of bad houses and bad roads in Ooty, and possibly he left no doubt that, as its first and leading citizen, he was exceedingly aggrieved. The bottled-up resentment of his colleagues came to a head in the reply from the Governor, which also seems to have been made public and survives in its un-diluted forthrightness, even brutality. For whatever tire-some characteristics can be guessed behind the complacency of that large egglike face, Mr. Sullivan had started here from scratch. He had coped with a multitude of difficulties before anyone else had come on the scene. The Governor, however, opens with a punishing broadside at his preten-sions to be the 'discoverer' of Ootacamund by saying that in his view the lively Mr. Whish and Mr. Kindersley have as good a right to that title as has the Collector, and he adds that 'the benefits derived from Mr. Sullivan's resi-dence at Ootacamund are not so very obvious and so generally acknowledged as to make it a matter of just surprise that they should now be called in question'. The Right Honourable the Governor 'would not have thought it necessary to have entered into detail upon the subject if

34

Mr. Sullivan had not called for the public gratitude in a tone of confidence that could not be passed over'. In the eighteen months since Ooty has been placed under a Military Commandant, the Governor bitingly observes, the roads and bazaars have improved more than in the eight years that Mr. Sullivan was in control of them. And the Governor has not finished yet. Now comes a sharp slap at the years that Sullivan has spent up here in Ooty, as though dallying in bed with a seductive mistress when he should have been looking after the neglected affairs of Coimbatore, his legal spouse. 'Indeed, the excess of the local affection which they [the Nilgiri Hills] inspire in those whose public duties require their presence elsewhere is the only public evil that has arisen from their discovery, and of this, Mr. Sullivan, the "first settler" '—the very fluid in the inkwell of the Governor's secretary seems acidulated—'has been the first and most enduring example.' Finally, that bland face is dunked into the waters of his own lake and held there. 'There is, however, one ground of local merit to which the Right Honourable the Governor feels that Mr. Sullivan may prefer an exclusive claim. He did what no one but the Collector could have done when he enlarged the bounds of a natural lake near Ootacamund by making a mud bank forty yards long across the farther end of it.'

It is a good, if nasty, exercise in the British art of being courteously lethal, and an astonishing revelation of dislike for a man. One can imagine the hum of gossip and laughter that it must have caused in Ooty and Coimbatore and Madras. Of its reception up at Stonehouse we know nothing. After 1830, Mr. Sullivan does not seem to have been so frequently in Ooty. He was made a member of the Council in Madras in 1835, and he retired from the service in 1840. Silence closes down. Five years later, he sold his house to a Major Macmurdo, who was, ironically enough, the Military Commandant at the time. The love affair was over. Mr. Sullivan must have quit India a

wealthy man, and an unusually healthy one, but he left his
wife, Henrietta, and two daughters behind lying in the
graveyard of St. Stephen's. 'Founder of Ootacamund' is the
inscription beneath his picture, and in spite of the Governor's savage attack, it appears to be the just one.

*

One beautiful morning, I try to find Mr. Sullivan's house,
or what remains of it. The hill on which it stands ascends
from Charing Cross, in the centre of which there is a
brightly painted memorial fountain, ornamented with
pagan-looking naked little boys and leering, bearded satyr
masks, which turns out, surprisingly, to commemorate a
Victorian Governor of Madras. Buses packed to the brim
with joggling turbans, and little pony traps, and noisy
trucks with men hanging on cheerfully to every inch of
their space, and ancient, sputtering cars, and Ooty's
often equally ancient cream-and-black taxis, all hooting
stridently, as though competing for a hundred-rupee prize
for the greatest din, career out of the converging roads
towards this landmark, apparently intending to flatten it
to the ground but circumventing it somehow and rattling
away. The fountain is not playing. It used to, as the little
guidebook I bought yesterday at Higginbotham's informs
me, when the rain gods were in good humour, but they
have not been in good humour for a long while, and last
year they turned their faces away disastrously from all
India, so that the monsoon failed and there are provinces
where famine is said to be not far distant. Rice is rationed
at a meagre four ounces a day for each person in Ooty, as
it is everywhere, and the wonderful new dam out on the
Wenlock Downs (the fifty-three square miles of gently
rolling bumps on the Mysore side of the town that are
named for another Governor), which is mentioned with so
much pride as an important part of Ooty's future, is at the
moment a mere puddle of green water, and the electric
light, I have noticed, is weak and sometimes expires

36

altogether, and the taps run as though in the charge of the smallest of the rain gods, a petulant, parsimonious boy. Grimly silent though the fountain stands, the general effect of Charing Cross is gay. A little farther on, Mahatma Gandhi sits—a golden bust of him on a pedestal under his own little roof—and beams benevolently at the passengers disgorging from the panting town bus with their bundles and babies and one or two thin, silent hens, carried nonchalantly by the feet, like handbags.

Up on Sullivan's hill, the noise dies away. Steps have been cut in the grassy slope, so that you can leave the looping motor road and take a short cut to the top, where the trees wave and whisper in the breeze. Stopping to get my breath, I remember the delightful letter that Sir Thomas Munro, the first Governor of Madras to visit Ooty, which he did in 1826, wrote to his wife in England, describing for her 'the numberless green knolls of every shape and size . . . as smooth as the lawns in an English park'. I can still see from this slope what he must have seen (though houses have sprouted from the knolls in all directions), and the turf has a wonderful plushy softness to the feet. A policeman pounding along the road in his heavy boots jerks his head amiably when I ask him the way to Stonehouse.

'This Stonehouse Hill.'

'But the *house* called Stonehouse?'

Perplexed, he stops a passerby. Several more people stop and join the discussion, which grows animated. We are the centre of quite a group, swollen by five or six children and a cow.

'Sullivan?' Nobody knows.

A stout man in a tweed jacket and a little round red cap, grasping a large umbrella, hurries down the road towards us. He is wreathed in friendly smiles. 'Are you possibly requiring assistance in locating some person or residence?' he asks.

But he shakes his head, disappointed with me when I go

on about an old house, Stonehouse, where Mr. Sullivan, the first European, used to live, and the arguments break out again. The fat man has the hopeful air of being able to supply any and every other bit of local information that I might like to ask. This one stumps him, however. 'Nobody called Sullivan living on Stonehouse Hill.'

So I give up Stonehouse for that day. Instead, wandering on over this delicious springy hilltop, with two or three little boys and the cow tagging along to see if anything develops, I almost literally stumble upon the ghost of a tiny lost cemetery that lies in a dip in the ground, so that the unwary walker comes near to taking a header into it over the crumbling remains of its low wall. I am told later that this is the oldest graveyard in Ooty, where the first civilian settlers and soldiers and their families were buried; it must have been a short stroll away from Mr. Sullivan's elusive Stonehouse. But nothing much survives now. There are only three or four anonymous tombs— from which the inset inscriptions have been removed, for some reason—sagging in ruin among the weeds and the rubbish. The cow steps daintily through a gap in the wall and begins morosely pulling at some rusty shrub beside the only tomb that can, with some difficulty, be read. It is a big stone box, with its flaking, worn inscription like an address on the lid; the little boys helpfully dust it with their fingers and chase off a basking lizard. 'Here lies the body of Henry Harington, Cornet in the 7th Regiment Light Cavalry, youngest son of the late William Harington Esquire of the Madras Civil Service, died on 22nd April 1823, in his 18th year.'

The Sullivans, I suppose, would have just settled down in their newly built house and would have been talking about getting their son christened the following month when Cornet Harington came up here, perhaps on leave from his regiment, took sick, and died, thus setting the pattern for the many British who were to come to Ooty and never leave. The cemetery is a queer, haunting little

38

spot, which will probably have sunk quietly without a trace into India in a few more years if no one does anything to preserve it, and few of the European residents to whom I mentioned it later had ever climbed up to see it, even if they knew vaguely where it was. That is always the way, they said. Visitors tell you of these things, but the people who live in a place are too busy. Modern Ooty has forgotten Mr. Sullivan, and soon his hill will be entirely given over—as it is today, except for that one faint voice from the past—to the cows, the barefooted little boys, and the young men and women students from the nearby College of Arts (once the Government Secretariat buildings), whose voices and cheerful laughter I hear in the distance as some of them stroll, the saris of the girls charmingly fluttering, under its trees.

PART THREE

My hotel, Willingdon House, is named for a former Vicereine who is reported to have left a trail of her favourite colour, mauve, across the sub-continent, just as that famous name has certainly left a trail of itself through Ooty. Before the building was a hotel—between the World Wars, I think—it was a sort of holiday hostel, organized by Lady Willingdon, where civil servants came to stay and restore themselves in the Nilgiri air. There is the Lady Willingdon Home for old ladies, Indian and European, in Ooty, and the former Assembly Rooms are now an English-language movie house bearing the name. The Willingdons' pictures still hang in the cinema entrance hall—black-and-white reproductions of portraits, Lord Willingdon painted by Oswald Birley, Lady Willingdon by de Laszlo—and very strange fish they look among the lurid advertisements for Westerns and not very recent American comedies. The management has also retained several framed photographs left over from the British days of amateur dramatics produced there—in the early twenties, I should say—and Indians who come in to study the movie stills sometimes linger to gaze gravely or with fits of laughter at these jolly groups of juvenile leads in tennis flannels, and colonels' wives hoping they look like Lily Elsie, and comic maids twirling feather dusters.

If there was ever anything mauve about the decoration of Willingdon House, it has vanished, but the interior is indubitably English, with bright cretonnes and big armchairs and old copies of the *Field*, and mounted elephant tusks, and Winston Churchill jutting out his jaw at the end of a passage, and, on other walls, the Queen (Trooping-the-Colour version) and palely talented watercolours of the Nilgiris and some spirited hunting pictures of the school that depicts pink coats falling, fallen, or convivially clinking something. The old butler, who has been here thirty-five years, does the flowers, bunching them together in shallow bowls with the instinctive style and eye for pure colour that so many Indians seem to possess, whether it is an ancient scarecrow walking along wearing a length of screaming cerise stuff flung round his skinny body with a panache that Balenciaga might envy and El Greco would have liked to paint, or the poorest woman squatting in the market behind an elegant little diagram of vegetables. I see the butler flitting round the garden in his long grey coat picking his flowers after he has served breakfast, which has (for appetites that can manage it) an Edwardian amplitude. There is no food shortage in Ooty except for rice. I am invited to consume a slice of papaya, then porridge, and after that a couple of fish cakes, perhaps, and surely, he suggests hopefully, a boiled egg or two, washed down with coffee and topped up with relays of toast and excellent home-made bitter marmalade. At lunchtime, he and the other servants change into smart sashed green coats with brass buttons, matching their turban bands. Lunch is hearty, too, but at four o'clock my room bearer rushes along a tea tray supplied with scones and jam or chopped-coriander sandwiches and Madeira cake to keep body and soul together until dinner at eight. Along with the scones arrives the dark sweeper girl, who pads in and builds pyramids of eucalyptus wood in the narrow, sunken fireplaces of my rooms and lights them by throwing herself down and blowing with a loud hissing noise into last night's ashes until a spark flares up and the gummy, aromatically scented wood catches.

The main hotel building is a rambling Victorian structure,

44

its separate bungalow wings connected by long, roofed-in veranda passages, over which a bougainvillaea and an orange-trumpeted creeper that I am told brings good fortune hurl themselves riotously, and along which at night the local cats often stalk, clattering loose tiles, filling the air with hoarse contralto growls and bronchitic love calls. By day, I sometimes encounter them—mere tabby shapes now, and not raging maenads—taking surfeited afternoon naps under the great scarlet geraniums that climb my veranda pillars. The rooms are enormously lofty, their corrugated-tin ceilings soaring to a steep point, like the roof of a Non-conformist chapel, and supported by a stout central beam that inquisitive small birds out of the garden sometimes use as a convenient perch for a beady-eyed examination of the new boarder. I notice that all the old houses in Ooty have been built on these spacious lines of British India, designed to shut out the blazing sun and encourage cool cross-currents of air; in a place where temperatures drop after dark like a stone for several months of the year, the plan seems less good. In my bedroom, the only windows are set very high in the walls, so that at night the room is like a cave lit by firelight, from which I can look up at rectangles of splendidly blazing stars that pale reluctantly as the faint light of the late-winter dawn announces that the sun is struggling up slowly on its long journey to Ooty from the plains. I find it difficult to sleep here because of the altitude, and Dr. R. Baikie, a former Medical Officer in Ooty who wrote an enthusiastic guidebook and medical manual for invalid visitors in 1834, mentions insomnia as a possible inconvenience for newcomers. It is one of the few adverse effects that he cares to admit in a spot that can, he claims, fix up practically everything in the way of human ills, bar 'the atrophy of advanced years, consequent upon long residence in the country and *Indianized habits*', which I take to be searing curries every day, washed down by the large quantities of claret, port wine, and sherry that the Victorian visitors to Ooty seem to have consumed. 'To

45

such unhappy subjects,' the Doctor observes sadly, 'after almost any degree of preparation, cold acts as a complete *extinguisher.*' I think of Dr. Baikie as I retrieve a slipping eiderdown and listen to the cats, whom I sometimes wish someone would extinguish, and to a distant jackal howling among the hills, which sets up a shuddery yelling from every dog in the town. The red eye of the remains of the fire opens and shuts companionably, and, watching it, I reflect drowsily how odd it is to have to come all the way to modern India to experience the house-party pleasures of a Victorian novel—firelight on the walls, and the reviving pot of strong tea, coddled inside a knitted cosy, brought noiselessly to the bedside in the morning, and the bath water trickling slowly into the galvanized hip-tub, and the sizzling breakfast kidneys and bacon that will probably, one can but feel, be followed by devilled pheasant legs and a grilled bone. The furniture is constructed on a scale to match the other props of this period piece in which I find myself dreamily moving. My nylons drop softly out of sight into a tall wicker dirty-clothes hamper that could swallow the laundry of a sahib and his whole family, and there are three wardrobes in my room—each one smelling mustily of the Orient and designed to take racks of sweeping muslins, and serge walking skirts, and hats with huge crowns to accommodate splendid coiled masses of hair—which have digested my clothes among them with distinctly irritable expressions of being on short rations.

The owner of my hotel, the celebrated Miss Guthrie, is one of the long-established residents of Ooty, for she ran the place for Lady Willingdon in the old days when its guests were civil servants. It is no good asking how many years she has been here; vagueness about time seems to be characteristic of many people in Ooty, and perhaps may be classed as an Indianized habit. Asked the same question, another Ooty lady answers cheerfully that she cannot quite recall, but 'I was here before the Todas arrived, definitely.' Miss Guthrie has been here a long while, one can say with certainty, and she is known throughout the Nilgiris, and down in Bangalore, where she keeps a few race horses, and far beyond. 'There were some Americans here not long ago who said they'd heard of me from some people in Spain,' she tells me with satisfaction. She screws up her eyes, and her pink face gets pinker after a wheeze of delighted laughter. She is a heavily built woman with red hair pulled back into a small knob, and she moves around slowly but purposefully on two sticks (she had a bad fall a few years ago), seeing to everything, missing nothing, issuing orders in a surprisingly small, piping treble voice that seems to belong to a different woman altogether. When Miss Guthrie appears, it is like an Army inspection visit; the staff start running about. However sharp the air may be, she dresses invariably in flowered cotton frocks with short sleeves. 'I'm warm-blooded, that's why,' she says. 'Not like Miss Myers. Miss Myers feels the cold.'

I and Miss Myers, the only permanent resident at Willingdon House at the moment, do not see much of Miss Guthrie. She has built herself a small, bright cottage, out of sight at the foot of the garden, where she lives with her elderly ayah, her budgerigars, her silver racing cups, photographs and sketches of her horses, and the *Madras Mail* opened at the racing page. It is an absorbing enthusiasm, which she developed as a sort of recompense after her accident. These beautiful speedy creatures run for her by proxy. She won several major races in her first season as an owner, and she aspires to carry off one or two big classic events of the Indian turf. At the moment, she is waiting with excitement for news of a favourite mare that is due to foal shortly down in Bangalore. When the wire comes, she will be off to look the new arrival over. On Wednesday evenings, she always has a few regular friends in to play canasta—an Indian woman doctor, a young Frenchman (one of the French technicians who have been for many months in Ooty installing the machinery in a big new film factory that has gone up, to the horror of the old

European residents, out on the beautiful Wenlock Downs), and one or two others. A stream of friends, Indian and European, turn up all the time to see her, and she keeps in touch with many retired service people back in U.K.—that curiously mythical spot—some of whose children are her godchildren and in any case send affectionate messages to 'Auntie Bunny'. Nine years or so ago, she went home and made a round of visits among old Willingdon House devotees, then she bought a car, hired a chauffeur, and 'did' the Continent in solitary state. 'Saw everything,' she says—Europe got an inspection visit, too. The car was shipped back to Ooty, and, writing on my veranda some mornings, I see Miss Guthrie depart in it for the market, sitting in the front seat beside her careful white-haired Tamil driver so that she can stretch out her bad leg, with Anthony, her major-domo—a rather melancholy-looking man never seen without his little round red plush cap—sitting at the back. She waggles a hand graciously in my direction, like Queen Mary.

Everyone in Ooty seems to know, and Miss Guthrie herself frequently mentions, that she intends to give up the hotel business 'when I can get my price—I'm in no hurry'. When that happens, she proposes to retire to her cottage and become a private citizen of Ooty with a keen interest in racing. This will leave the Ooty Club and the Savoy Hotel, up at the same end of the town, and one or two smaller guest-houses as the only surviving establishments where the direction is still European. Even a newcomer may speculate that the exacting game of running a hotel cannot be as good as it was, now that Ooty's really prosperous days as a hill station—a good-time girl to whom the British kept coming back for a century and a quarter—are surely over. Hill stations in India must have begun to decline, anyway, when air travel home to U.K. became popular. Though the better-off Indians may have picked up the habit of going to the hills from the British, the Government does not move up here from Madras *en bloc*

48

for several months, as the British used to do, and if the hotels are booked solid for the season, the season is short, and I note becalmed pages in the visitors' book at Willingdon House. Just now, I am the only guest except for the permanent Miss Myers. An Indian party shows up briefly —several excited little boys cheeping like a nest of sparrows, and their mothers in sporty sweaters and tight scarlet slacks—and a British doctor and his wife from Mysore arrive with their children, whom they are taking back to school in Ooty, where parents from many parts of India and Ceylon send their young to imbibe education and healthy air in equal parts. The Mysore family look washed out and tired when they arrive, especially the parents, but in a couple of days they all have such a restored appearance that I cannot fail to imagine Dr. Baikie's devoted shade hovering in satisfaction around his professional colleague's table, watching the children as they tuck into their porridge.

But for most of the time Miss Myers and I sit alone at our little tables facing each other across the big dining-room, while the grave clock ticks behind me, and the green-uniformed figures serve us with dignity, and our voices, making the small talk of people who meet in a hotel, boom and tangle confusingly in the echoing recesses of the high ceiling. Miss Myers is a former principal of St. Mary's College, Madras, who made her home here after she retired from government service—'years and years ago', she says with a short laugh, giving the vague Ooty specific for time. Now she is honorary secretary of the Nilgiri Library—a tall, rather severe red brick building with an air of North Oxford about its white-trimmed ecclesiastical windows and its *porte-cochère*, beyond the tourist office and the Chinese shoemaker and the silversmith, who, rather surprisingly in this 'dry' Indian state, displays a silver-plated cocktail shaker and an ice bucket in his window, along with other fixtures of gracious living. Like the Library, Miss Myers' face, with its bright, intelligent eyes looking out from under a low fringe of straight bobbed hair, is of a type that would be at home in Oxford, where, as a young woman, she took her degree in English at St. Hilda's. Her family were all connected with India (one relative was an eminent cleric in Madras), and she was educated as a child up here in Ooty in the Nazareth Convent, but she still talks occasionally of the possibility that she may go 'home' for good one day to U.K., where she has a sister. We talk of the Tate Gallery and the British Museum, and of a nice little hotel, conveniently situated for buses and tubes, where she stays when she returns to visit, and of the joys of the fruit department of Marks & Spencer. Oh, the flavour of those big Jaffa oranges at home! How superior to the (to me perfectly delicious) little Indian fruit that comes in a loose, fragrant overcoat several sizes too big for it. The Kashmir apples, huge and rosy, look so beautiful that they might be the first of their kind invented by God, but they are dust and ashes in Miss Myers' opinion, compared to a good Kent-grown Cox's Orange Pippin. To her mind, all this Eastern fruit is extremely overrated. Every week, she goes down to the market, buys a large bunch of plantains, and hangs them up in her bathroom so that they can ripen 'properly' under her eye. And what is better than a Royal Sovereign strawberry, firm and perfect, with a port-wine flush, or a White Heart cherry of the old kind that you had to take two or three bites to? English orchards surround us, foaming in pink and white, as we eat our mangoes.

Miss Myers drives the short distance to her Library every morning in her Standard car, sailing out dashingly into the road with a peremptory toot of the horn among the passing bicyclists and bullock carts and the fruit peddler and his cronies who squat permanently near the gate. She runs the Library with great efficiency, keeping in touch with the literary life through the *Observer* and the *Times Literary Supplement*, which assist her to order the monthly parcel of books from London; she follows contemporary topics in the other English periodicals that come regularly into the reading room. The B.B.C. is also a great bridge between the Nilgiris and U.K. After dinner, she retires punctually to her room to listen to the calm Britannic voice of the Overseas Programme news reader giving tidings of Mr. Wilson and Rhodesia and the Queen through what, on nights when reception is bad, sounds like the waves of all the oceans rolling along from the Straits of Dover to break in thunder on the Malabar coast.

Miss Myers' own cultivated, resonant voice is pitched to issue orders and address assembled students, and her punctuality is famous among all her friends in Ooty. The timetable habit prevails. A sort of personal class bell seems to ring in her mind, denoting the end of a period. Soon I begin to know what hour it is by noticing when Miss Myers folds up her table napkin, or issues forth on her constitutional, or returns from the Club, where she plays bridge always on certain evenings. She is interested in many things in Ooty, and between these activities, the Library, bridge, and much reading, she 'passes the time' by embroidering the brilliant little needlework pictures that she diffidently shows me one morning in her room. They are delicate copies in silks ('But it's hard nowadays to get really good colours in Ooty') of anything she fancies—a Mogul painting of horsemen scampering along in flowery meadows, a Chinese scroll, or (at the moment not quite finished) two of Matisse's odalisque women with a vase of pure orange and pink flowers. One of the day's periods, at least, must be marked 'Exercise'. When she has returned from the Library and put the car away in its garage in the servants' compound, she issues out again on foot, holding a sunshade carefully over her head, to which, if the sun is particularly burning, she may give the added protection of a round-brimmed pink cotton hat. And every evening on the dot her spare, youthfully energetic figure in its tweed suit crosses the lawn of Willingdon House and can be encountered later loping along pretty fast on one of the roads or hill tracks under the eucalyptus trees and the wattles, with their feather mops of fluffy palest-yellow bloom, taking the customary walk that is usually succeeded in the schedule by 'Bridge'.

Miss Myers drives me over to the Library one morning, and I become a temporary member by paying five rupees to the elderly Indian librarian, who sits behind a counter off the hall with his assistant, a smiling little lady who generally has her outdoor coat draped round her shoulders against the cold as she stamps the books, and who tells me, with innumerable ecstatic flutterings and weaving of her narrow hands, of the wonderful three years she spent some time ago in Richmond, U.K. Ah, Richmond! The buses, the River Thames, the rain—— but the librarian returns just then from speaking to Miss Myers in her office, and the assistant patters off busily with a pile of the newest books. There is no more fruitful place, except perhaps the Club, in which to begin a gentle stroll through Ooty's past than the lofty Reading Room, with its five big arched windows on each side and a tall Gothic window at the far end; its round tables laid out with magazines and newspapers; its pictures of Elizabeth and, for good measure, Philip; its green-shaded library lamps and faded matting and shabby rep-covered armchairs cosily shaped by I do not know how many decades of slumped forms; its smell of India. The stuffed heads of a Nilgiri sambar stag and a bison look down on the tranquil scene, and I am slightly startled by a horrific mask of a moth-eaten bear, snarling out of a Beatle shag of matted hair over the double doors through which I have just entered; the passage of time and slight damage to his nose have given him a balefully human expression.

I wander around dipping into the extraordinarily well-stocked glass-fronted cases of new biography and travel and fiction, and look at the *Times of India* and flick through an *Illustrated London News*. It is a disappointment to find that there is no local paper, for local papers are generally as full of clues to a place as all the guidebooks put together.

Miss Myers tells me later that there used to be one—the *Nilgiri Gazette,* which was printed across the way from the Library. It did not survive Independence, and an earlier journal, the *Eclectic & Nilgiri Chronicle,* pegged out in 1861, in spite of the dubious success of a first number containing a brilliant article, said to have been written by one of the officers stationed in Ooty, which turned out to have been lifted entire from Isaac D'Israeli's 'Curiosities of Literature'. I sit reading by a notice sternly demanding 'Silence!' but the Library does not altogether obey, being dry in its joints from long exposure to the thin Nilgiri air. Every now and then, it sighs and lets out an arthritic creak from its floorboards, and the matting lifts slightly, the bear's coiffure seems to bristle still more modishly in the draught from the opening of the double doors as a member enters—a European lady, who passes lightly and rapidly down the room like a phantom from the twenties, girlishly erect, her wide hat and her parasol and her resolutely pink-and-white complexion suggesting that the far door through which she disappears must lead, not to another part of the Library, as I afterwards learn it does, but to the painted set of a deanery garden, where other guests, drinking China tea and eating cucumber sandwiches, are admiring the Dean's delphiniums. Presently, a military-looking man comes in to read the newspapers, and a pretty young girl in a tangerine sari lingers along the shelves of novels, sampling and hesitating like a butterfly undecided whether to settle on a fine, large Daphne du Maurier or to explore the more complex heart of a 'modern' variety—a Muriel Spark or an Iris Murdoch.

The Nilgiri Library was built in 1868 from the design of a Mr. Chisholm at a cost of thirty-eight thousand rupees, and it seems to have become a favourite meeting place right away, as it is today for the remnants of the European residents. Edward Lear, when he was in Ootacamund in 1874, consumed a breakfast of beefsteak and claret directly he arrived, went for a walk, and, observing everything with those marvellously sharp, amused little eyes behind the thick spectacles, noted apprehensively 'a vast many carriages outside the Library' and a multitude of smart turnouts everywhere, with two uniformed *syces* perched at the back. All the tokens, he sighed to his journal, indicated that 'some martyrdom at the Governor's' was inevitable. And, sure enough, Lady Hobart, the Governor's lady, swooped down on him and got him 'to promise to drive tomorrow, and lunch: woe is me!'

I do not know which discovery astonishes me more—the richness of the Library's contents or the information that, all told, it has only about fifty members, Indian and European in the whole of Ooty. Perhaps the other bookish people who live here use the public library, which is free, or borrow volumes from the shelves of the Ooty Club, or get along on a diet of the paperbacks—thrillers with erotic covers mixed up with Shaw and the Karmasutra and manuals on the right etiquette for every social occasion— that are on sale in Higginbotham's. At any rate, the Library has long been genteelly pinched for cash, and it is only very recently, I learn, that the managing committee, which has a prominent Ooty resident, Sir C. P. Ramaswami Aiyar,* as chairman, decided to take a step to improve its financial position. It has sold a bare half acre of ground immediately alongside the Library to the municipality for sixty-three thousand rupees—a price that would certainly make Mr. Sullivan sit up if he could compare it with the one rupee an acre tariff that the Todas were offered for their buffalo pastures. On the site, a town hall is due to rise, at some date that most people consider highly problematical, considering the serious national financial difficulties. The idea of a town hall is a novelty to Ooty. Some of the Library members who wish that the place could stay exactly as it is deplore the eventual loss of their absolute peace and privacy, and dislike the prospect of municipal typewriters, in defiance of the 'Silence!' notice, chattering

* See p. 101.

MEET OF THE
OOTACAMUND
HUNT, 1896.
Reproduced by kind
permission of the
Hon. Mrs. C. Fortescue

GROUP AT GOVERNMENT HOUSE: OPENING OF THE OOTACAMUND HUNT, 1903

out of the next-door windows, but they cannot deny that the spacious scale of the old Victorian planners has proved a life-saver.

The real wealth of the Library is, anyway, not on its balance sheet or on view in the mellow Reading Room. It is cached away, as I soon discovered, upstairs on the floor where the stacks climb to the ceiling, and in two upper rooms in that part of the building towards which the Dean's tea-party guest had proceeded. Very few people seem to come to these rooms; on most days the inquirer into the history of Ootacamund can pull the library steps from shelf to shelf and browse undisturbed, dusty and happy. For here are the bare bones of British India— transactions of the East India Company, official records of Fort St. George, the trading settlement founded by the Company in 1640 on the site of modern Madras, from its early days, histories of the Mutiny, reports on the administration of the Nilgiris, faded folios of charts and maps, privately printed calculations of barometric readings and geological deposits and tribal movements across the sub-continent, and scholarly disquisitions on the Vedanta philosophy and Rajput ballads and Hindu heroes by men in love with India. Here are the complete gazeteers of districts, and slim, yellowing reports put together by dead and gone Political Agents of the intrigues and splendours of the native princes, and a folder of delightful watercolour sketches by a major-general of the Madras Army in the sixties of sahibs in topees draped with veils or in turbaned felt 'wide-awakes' strolling on the peaceful hills beside their dressy *mem-sahibs* in bustles and tight Zouave jackets, with smart pill-box toques perched above netted chignons. I enjoy looking through the items of a deceased Englishman's effects sold at public auction somewhere in Madras State, which include '3 Wiggs, 17 short Drawers, 24 Elephant's teeth, 1 tubb of Europe butter, and a Lump of Books', and I sample gossipy memoirs of Governors' ladies and glance admiringly into the many-volumed life works of affectionate specialists on the flowers, trees, wild animals, birds, butterflies, and reptiles of South India. This section is the place for leisurely research into some of the Library's treasures, but my favourite retreat is the Wardrop Room, named after some benefactor about whom nobody seems to know anything except that he was a general—a perfect piece of old Ooty preserved, where one can sit and read in its pleasant, musty silence, surrounded by bound complete sets of *Punch,* the *Edinburgh Review, Blackwood's,* and *Vanity Fair* and Dickens' *Household Words,* under the not unfriendly gaze of whiskered gentlemen who were former secretaries of the Library. Over the mantelpiece hangs a portrait in oils 'Painted for the Inhabitants of Ootacamund to Commemorate the Jubilee of Her Majesty, Queen Victoria, Empress of India, 1887'. The fat little face with its arched nose and heavy-lidded blue eyes pouts petulantly in the general direction of the proposed town hall. On one or two dull afternoons, when the low clouds hold a purple umbrella over Dodabetta, the big mountain, and the Library talks away to itself in the total quiet, I have spent several enjoyable hours in one of a pair of absolutely elephantine worn black leather armchairs that stand, or kneel, side by side before Queen Victoria with an expectant air of waiting for literary types to arrive and be hoisted up into their vast, sagging howdahs.

PART FOUR

I T is no distance from my hotel to the Ootacamund Club, the principal rallying spot for the dwindled band of Europeans in the Nilgiris. The Club is European in its direction, and until a few years ago it was exclusively European in its membership. Now all this is altered, but though today the Club welcomes members from both communities, and the ubiquitous Sir C. P. Ramaswami Aiyar is its vice-president, the Indians do not seem to use it much. I am told that this is not so in the April and May season, when the Race Weeks bring owners and trainers and the gay younger sons of Indian princes (the sporting set whom Dennis Kincaid, in his 'British Social Life in India', quoted as beginning new acquaintanceships by asking, 'What games do you play—besides golf and tennis, I mean?') flocking into Ooty. But in this quieter time of its engagement book, which I suspect is nowadays 'the real Ooty', I do not see any Indians sitting in companionable groups on the blue-and-white-linen-covered sofas, or having a peg in the bar, or lunching in the panelled dining-room. 'Indians don't long for intercourse with Englishmen any more,' wrote E. M. Forster in 'The Hill of Devi'. 'They have made a life of their own.' And they seem to prefer (at least in Ooty) to pursue it at their own clubs— the Lawley Institute and the Indian Union, a sympathetic but ghostly old building that returns the compliment by allowing European members. Perhaps the long years of segregation have not been entirely forgotten or forgiven.

A beautifully proportioned low white building, its wings spreading on either side of a classical pillared portico, the Ooty Club sits gracefully on a steep knoll that is approached by an avenue of venerable trees, to one side of which a grove of wild arum lilies springs out of a marshy cleft in the ground. The building has been much altered—though the pillared frontage, I think, was part of the original design—since Sir William Rumbold built it in the eighteen-twenties. He was a rich, polished, and unfortunate young man whose family had strong roots in India; his grandfather, Sir Thomas Rumbold, had been Governor of Madras at the end of the eighteenth century. His childhood must have been conditioned by talk of the East India Company and by the intoxicating smells of the teak chests in which the silks and spices and the elephants' tusks were brought home by voyaging relatives. Having married, at the age of twenty-two, an eighteen-year-old heiress, the daughter of Lord Rancliffe, he brought his wife out to India in 1813 in the hope of amassing a still greater fortune. He was amiable and highly accomplished, and the young couple cut a great dash, but things went wrong for him. He became a partner in William Palmer & Co., a mercantile and banking firm in Hyderabad that financed the ruling Nizam. The firm finally failed, and Sir William's growing financial worries were further darkened by the loss of Lady Rumbold, who died in Ooty in 1830, giving birth to her seventh child. His extravagances, which had included the building of this elegant mansion in the Nilgiris, had been excessive, and, worn out and harassed, he followed her three years later, at the age of forty-six—not really a very short life for the British in those days, to judge by the average that is recorded on the tombstones in St. Stephen's. Many superstitious people in Ooty shook their heads as they recalled that his misfortunes piled up after he chose to build on especially sacred Toda ground—the site of one of their ancient temples.

Sir William's fine house, the best in the young settlement, became the home of visiting Governors, who started coming up to Ooty from Madras and showed such inclinations to linger there, enjoying the cool nights and the glorious brilliant days, that at least one of them (Lord Elphinstone, in 1840) was only reluctantly recalled to the oven of the plains after eight months of tart dispatches from the displeased authorities. Before that, it was the temporary headquarters of a Governor-General of India—the title, first held by Warren Hastings, which was changed to Viceroy when the administration of India was transferred from the East India Company to the Crown by Act of Parliament in 1858. Lord William Bentinck, the Governor-General from 1828 to 1835, was staying in Ooty and there greeted a new arrival from England in 1834. This was a short, stout, good-humoured man of thirty-three, with a noble head and a badly tied neckcloth, whose mind danced like marsh gas, who was adored by all children as an impassioned improviser of magnificent games and talker of nonsense language, and who was physically so clumsy that, as his nephew and biographer wrote later, he never succeeded in jamming more than the tips of his fingers into his shiny new kid gloves. Thomas Babington Macaulay's sturdy form had been lugged all the four hundred miles from Madras by palanquin, for he was no horseman and had once observed firmly, when staying at Windsor Castle and tipped off to be in attendance on the Queen's morning exercise, 'If Her Majesty wishes to see me ride, she will have to order up one of her elephants.' Newly elected by the directors of the East India Company as the first legal member of the Supreme Council and appointed to head the new commission to reform the law, he had been sailing to Calcutta with his sister Hannah, who was going out to keep house for him. But at Madras a messenger from the Governor-General came unexpectedly on board. Lord William had been recovering from an illness, it seemed, in Ootacamund—some newly discovered spot, Macaulay vaguely thought, 'in the mountains of Malabar, beyond

Mysore'—and was not yet fit to travel. Therefore, a meeting of the Supreme Council was about to be convened up there, to which the new English member was now summoned to post with speed, since it happened that a quorum could not be formed until he arrived. So Hannah sailed on alone towards Calcutta and the hospitality of a friend of their father's, kind Bishop Wilson. Macaulay jogged off to Ooty, travelling in the more tolerable cool of the nights, resting in the heat of the day, and breaking his journey at Bangalore to stay with a Colonel Gubbon, who told his guest pathetically on departure that it had been the pleasantest three days he had passed in thirty years. He made another halt at Seringapatam to see Tippu Sultan's fortress and ruined palace—its courts, he noted, already disappearing, as the little British cemetery on Stonehouse Hill is sinking today, into the oblivion of India's indiscriminately tolerant wild flowers and trees. Then, having met nobody but monkeys on the road, he peered out of his palanquin as the party rounded a bend, and saw the first English cottages. Soon his servants were unpacking his luggage and 'coughing round' him 'in all directions', as he wrote to a friend.

Macaulay stayed in Ooty from June to September, and the time went slowly. It rained without cease, and the company was poor to one who had come fresh from Holland House, where he was used to finding himself dining in a party with, say, Lord Grey and Lord Palmerston, and Talleyrand might look in later, and Canning's beautiful daughter, Lady Clanricarde, would talk brilliantly, though 'with a little more of political animosity than is quite becoming in a pretty woman', and, after the evening ended, Lord John Russell would probably offer a lift back to London, and more conversation, in his cabriolet. The Ooty worthies were an intolerably dull exchange. The place was raw and new, and Macaulay was bored by flowers and did not care for nature in the wild, where you could be 'trod into the shape of a half-crown by a wild ele-plant, or eaten by the tigers', which came up to the hills, he said, for the same reasons that had brought him and many an Englishman to India: 'They encounter an uncongenial climate for the sake of what they can get.' But every newcomer to Ooty is told the proud local tradition that it was here, sitting in his cottage alongside the old Rumbold house while the monsoon rain rushed down the hill, that Macaulay began making the first notes for his great Indian Penal Code.

The Ootacamund Club appears to have been given no fresh, revitalizing shot from the present, as has the Wellington Gymkhana Club, twelve miles of corkscrew twists down the valley at Coonoor, where the young officers stationed at the barracks there come to play golf and tennis and, together with their attractive wives, to dance on gala nights. The new Indian Army Staff College stands on a rise not far away—a handsome building with the last word in modern equipment. In cabinets in the long mess are ravishing displays of some of the beautiful old state dinner services made for the East India Company. On its walls there are portraits of British military faces, under eighteenth-century wigs or modern service caps, which came along to their new home after partition, in the share-out of the pictures and mess silver of the old British Army Staff College in Quetta. When I go down to look round Coonoor, it seems to me that the few Europeans I see about the place look younger, too, than those I see in Ooty (where the accent is, to say the least, on maturity), and I guess that they are mostly planters from the tea estates, or connected in one way or another with the tea industry. The British imported the first bushes from China in the eighteen-fifties, and tea has been grown widely in the Nilgiris since then. There are still twenty-six British-owned estates left, and about fifteen British planters remain in the area.

But here in Ooty the only new blood that has come into the Club recently, it seems, has been an influx of French,

63

who for two years or so have been working to install the new Hindustan Photo Film factory and train Indians to run it. The project is being financed by the Government of India in collaboration with the French firm of Bauchet & Cie., and the new factory and its satellite buildings sprawl like a large white octopus on the Mysore side of Ooty, 'ruining' its loveliest stretch of country, as I hear continuously lamented by European acquaintances. All the unmarried Frenchmen have now moved into a recently completed hostel near the factory, and Ooty sees them less often. The planters come up regularly, though, for meetings or to play rugger or to have a fishing week-end in the hills, and they drop in frequently at the Club. In August, everybody in PASI, the Planters' Association of South India, musters in force, with wives, for Ooty's Planters' Week, and big dinner parties spread out over the dining-room, and the bar customers ignore the first booming dinner gong—and are likely to ignore the second, too—and the place hums with loud, cheerful voices. It is the jollification of the year, and everyone looks forward to it. I am shown the photographs of last Christmas's annual children's party, to which the guests also came from far and wide, when the lounge was transformed by the mothers into a really ambitious toy snowscape of cotton wool and frosting where wild animals roamed and cottage windows glimmered, and one of the fathers, dressed up in whiskers, distributed the presents to a jolly crowd of children, Indian and European, who were afterwards grouped, solemnly staring, for a picture out on the pillared front porch in the December sunshine.

But apart from such events the Club is encountering the hard times that are worrying club secretaries everywhere, all the way from St. James's Street to Ootacamund. The old subscription list of four hundred members is now rather less than half that. It surprises me, to tell the truth, that it is still so big, but people in many parts of the Nilgiris and beyond, I am told, belong to it. The ample staff of excellently trained servants has to be kept at full strength, or else, when the season is on and every man is needed, they will have gone off and got themselves jobs elsewhere. As though this were indeed St. James's Street, Ooty seems to be beginning to experience a situation in which skilled labour can pick and choose. Yet most of the time, though the attendant figures hover, the big rooms are empty, the comfortable armchairs drawn up in friendly groups appear, like those shabby, wistful elephants in the Wardrop Room, to be ready to receive the forms of members who do not come, and nobody sits at the writing tables freshly laid out with racks of the pale-green Club writing paper engraved with its crest of a Nilgiri sambar's antlers, and there is hardly a stampede to secure the air-mail London *Times* from the table where it lies crisply folded along with *Vogue* and the *Field*. A few couples may drop in for lunch or tea, and even in the quiet months a sprinkling of visitors come and stay in its comfortable old-fashioned bedrooms.

On Tuesday, Thursday, and Saturday afternoons there is, I have discovered, the same unvarying ritual in the lounge. After tea, one of the servants in his smart white uniform comes pattering along, appearing to breathe smoke like a dragon, for he is bearing a shovel filled with smouldering logs for the fireplace over in one corner. While he puffs them into flames, another servant sets out a card table and packs of cards. Presently, Mrs. Hill, the highly efficient Club secretary, appears. She is a quiet-voiced woman with cropped grey hair and an infinitely tolerant smile of amusement for the ways of Ooty, where she had been for many years. She dresses always in a tailored suit, and fishes up from its capacious pockets the replacements for her apparently eternal cigarette. On the tick of half past five ('You can set your watch by her'), Miss Myers strides in, flushed by her customary walk, and two other Ooty residents—a Mrs. Turner and a Mrs. Hildebrand—appear, and the four women sit down to

65

bridge. (On Mondays and Wednesdays, Miss Myers plays at the Indian Union Club, to which she also goes on Fridays for the meetings of the Culture Circle, a group that listens to speakers on various topics. This leaves only Sunday to be filled in between tea and dinner—by going, perhaps, to see 'some American trash' at the Assembly Rooms cinema.) This ladies' four is a fixture, always the same; the Club's men members, I take it, either do not play or have better things to do. The ladies' voices, conducting amiable post-mortems or exchanging scraps of gossip, echo through the room, where I sit glancing at *The Times* to assure myself that U.K. still exists somewhere, and sipping a gin-and-lime docked off my drink ration card, under the mournful gaze of several magnificent wild animal heads that gloom or show their enviable teeth from the walls. The bridge players do not order refreshments; the dark panelled bar remains dark and empty. Indians and Europeans join frequently in bewailing prohibition, which has so disastrously curtailed club and hotel conviviality, not to mention revenue. Except on special occasions, the Europeans prefer to drink their ration (four bottles of spirits a month) at home. But everyone has something to say on the subject—some bit of advice, or a warning story, or a really first-class recipe for making a delicious liqueur out of plums or bitter oranges. The Indian gin, they say, is the best. The Indian Scotch—a clan that one eyes somewhat doubtfully right from the start—is generally not appreciated by people fresh out from U.K., but real Scotch costs from seventy-five to one hundred rupees a bottle, and 'the only people who can afford that', a retired Englishman living up here in this haven of the pensioned tells me in the not unkindly tones that a hard-up aristo might use when mentioning the goings on of the vulgar new *dolce-vita* set, 'are rich millowners and suchlike down in Coimbatore or Bangalore.' For everybody who can afford it drinks now, he adds. 'Everybody' (except, of course, the strict adherents to religious principles) appears to be a registered 'addict' on medical grounds, and thus permitted to hold a ration sheet, or else a foreigner like me, to whom a tourist drink permit is issued in case I shake the dust of India off my feet in disgust if I cannot get a gin before dinner. As for the poor in Ooty, who can afford nothing, they drink as much as anybody. It's cold for them up here, poor devils, says the Englishman. They must have a nip of something. It would be all right if they could get some decent beer, as they used to do when We were here. But nowadays any-thing is said to go into these illicit home stills—a bit of paddy, a lot of fermented fruit, cleaning polish, the odd lizard or two, and an old electric-battery, perhaps, just to give the brew a bit of zip. Everyone has a warming, stupefying tot—the women and little children included— and you can hardly pick up a paper that does not contain some village item about a family drinking tragedy.

On one or two evenings when I do go into the bar of the Club, I feel that its atmosphere is a shade lugubrious, and that even a party of Coimbatore millowners spending like rajahs might have difficulty in bringing it to life. One of its difficulties as a place for lighthearted drinking is, I think, the surveillance by the gallery of wildlife on the walls, which here consists of two splendid tigers—both presented by a much loved old doctor, now dead, who was a crack shot and appears to have been called in if anything striped was seen strolling socially in the neighbourhood as automatically as he was summoned to diagnose a sud-den raging temperature—and a whole frieze of jackal masks. Jackals were hunted instead of foxes by the famous Ootacamund Hunt, and they still are, for this institution continues. Each of the specimens in the bar is mounted on a light wooden shield bearing the date of its final run, and the art of the taxidermist has cunningly varied the expres-sions of these antique, moulting trophies, so that one snarls out of the right side of the mouth, one out of the left, shabby ears are flattened or pricked, tongues loll or are nipped back *in extremis* between the teeth, with an effect

67

that I fancy all but truly sporting types might find a trifle unnerving after the third gin. These are 'real hill "jacks",' as a Victorian follower of the Ooty hounds affectionately lauded them—'very different from his mangy, sneaking brother of the plains'—and I try to reflect on their gallant qualities while avoiding the united glare of their glassy eyes.

When I go in to eat the Club's excellent food in the cosy dining-room, there is no getting away from the Horse. I am surrounded on all sides by enlarged photographs of past masters and huntsmen of the Ooty Hunt, sitting big and blue-eyed and walrus-moustached—though with a less vivacious range of expression than the jackals— on their beautiful horses. They look like portraits in rock that no tidal wave of history would be able to shift. The faces of these sportsmen, I make out as I eat my grilled cutlet, are solemn, and I think of a book I was reading recently in which someone observed reminiscently, 'I took India for granted as a boy, and also the fact that one was *there.*' We are *here*, say all these sometimes elongated but well-boned profiles staring confidently between their horses' ears. Perfectly turned out, sitting easily in the saddle, they look ahead, one fancies, into a glorious Nilgiri morning smelling of eucalyptus, and it must have seemed that it would last forever. In this room, the Horse is so overpoweringly present, the study of mostly dead-and-gone faces is so mesmerizing, that I can almost catch an ammoniacal whiff of the stables as I eat.

For further inquiry into the past, the Club has a rich selection of albums of yellowing photographs and newspaper clippings and hand-painted programmes of amateur theatricals and dance programmes with little pink pencils attached on fluffy silk cords. One learns that the Ooty Hunt began hunting 'jacks' with foxhounds in 1844, three years after the Club itself was started. Before that, a young and certainly intrepid Mr. Marriot used to invite other suicidal friends to go out with him shooting tigers and

68

sambar that were driven towards their guns by Marriot's 'bobbery pack'—a mixed bag of terriers, pointers, spaniels, setters, and mongrel pi-dogs of all kinds. The imported foxhounds that survived the journey from England did not always take to India. It used to be the custom to send them down to winter in Madras, where epidemics often ravaged the kennels; many of the hounds went blind before they died. Later, someone had the better idea of keeping the pack all the year round at Ooty, as they are kept today in kennels near the golf links. I enjoy the old photographs of meets on the lawns of large, well-kept houses—huge turnouts, with the ladies in tight-waisted habits poured over the bust and in topees or top hats circled coquettishly with flowing veils, and the small boy followers on their donkeys, and the maharajahs in Savile Row breeches, Lobb boots, and stunning turbans, and the dog-boys holding the terriers. As the years go on, nothing much alters but the shape of the women. We are here, all the tranquil faces continue to affirm. Has not Lord Randolph Churchill stated, 'We will never give up India'? Sometimes in the clippings from sporting journals the bright rattle of imitation English life falters, and India put a huge, thin, dusty foot in the door. It is 1854, and the popular 74th Highlanders have just arrived at the new barracks in Wellington and are hunting every Saturday. Everyone says that the amateur production of 'Box and Cox' is a scream. But suddenly the 74th disappears, and the theatricals lapse and are not revived for several years; the Mutiny has broken out. And in 1876, a year of terrible famine in the plains, the Governor and his Council and most of the menfolk are kept at their desks in Madras, though the correspondent of the London *Field* reports with a touch of malice, 'Ooty suffered no lack of life in consequence. . . . Gossip never flew so blithely, or reputations so lightly; tongues were no less glib; ears were no less open. Maidens were no more timid, matrons no less frisky, though fathers and husbands were not there to guard them, and the social wolf of India (who ever loves and never weds) beset their path at every turn.'

I read in the albums about Ooty characters such as Captain Ricardo of the 14th Hussars, nicknamed Chowey, whose *chota hazree* consisted invariably of an enormous glass of gin with a light dash of soda, and who arrived for his honeymoon in 1879 with a bag of 'overnight things' for himself and his bride, which turned out to be only eighteen pairs of riding boots. Then there was Major Bob Jago, who hunted the pack about the same date and was famous for his mighty bellow, which sent every sambar and pig scuttling out of the coverts, and who was hailed in a burst of verse by a local poet: 'Oh, it's jolly to hunt with the Nilgiri Pack, Major Bob with the horn and a straight-going "jack", etc., etc.' I admire photographs of pretty women with rows of tight curls arranged along their eyebrows like snail shells, who are in their turn admiring pawky little hunt terriers sitting, stiff-legged and condescending, in the lee of their braided skirts. I read the sad story of a huntsman—'a smart, well-made light fellow' called Elliot, who came out in the eighteen-sixties from the kennels of great Petworth House in Sussex, but had to be shipped home after taking to riotous living. There are lists of hounds reading like bucolic poetry; speedy Pardon, a splendid line-hunting type of Belvoir bitch; and keen and good Stormy; and famous old Pilgrim, from stalwart Vale of the White Horse ancestry; and Daffodil, fast and true but—alas, poor Daffodil—nearly mute. And there are records of the season's losses: Guardian vanished over a waterfall, Bonny chewed by a panther, Rambler a victim of rabies.

After 1914, there is a big hole in the air; a lot of the young men have disappeared over the waterfall, too. Then everything starts up with a bang; Ooty is her gay self again. The women, of course, are a different shape. Legs are in, hair is out; a chorus of shingled beauties link arms for the photographer after an amateur revue that was jolly nearly as good, all are agreed, as anything you could see in Shaftesbury Avenue when you went home on leave. Only men, horses, and hounds remain sturdily constant in appearance, and everyone is still riding, riding, as hard as he can go, hell for leather, through the twenties, uphill and downhill over the Downs after the lion-hearted 'jacks', into the thirties and the Second World War, when Ooty was full to bursting of people and gaiety for perhaps its last period of true renaissance. After 1947, the albums' shapes slim down also. The British have gone in large numbers, and the field is thinning out. A good-looking Indian M.F.H. leans cheerily out of his saddle to talk to somebody, and the Staff College officers are keen, and there are big crowds, as usual, for the point-to-point races on the Downs, when all Ooty turns out to enjoy itself. But now it may be that the Hunt is heading for extinction at last, having run full tilt into Progress, which has drawn a red chalk circle around Ootacamund on the map in some planner's office in Delhi.

Out of all India, Ooty was chosen four years ago as the site for the monster Hindustan Photo Film plant, which was to have cost eight crores (£6,000,000) under India's third Five Year Plan and has already, according to local talk, rung up eleven crores on the Government's cash register while still spreading itself out on the Downs. From a flurry of dusty building activity there are emerging a satellite town to lodge the workers, new roads along which the laden trucks rattle, and a handsome house perched on a ridge where the manager will live. In addition to manufacturing all manner of scientific film, I am told, this great place will ease India's anxious financial position by making cinema film, which has had to be imported in the past to feed the vast movie industry. Large numbers of people have already swarmed into Ooty in the hope of getting jobs when the plant eventually starts working. Then, a little while ago, there was talk of a radio telescope's also being built out on the Downs, but the site

71

appears to have been abandoned after a delegation of Todas complained that it would destroy one of their most sacred temples. And I hear rumours of an instant-tea factory, and perhaps a plant for the manufacture of some brand of baby foods.

Ooty, which was built and kept floating for so long as a place where people mostly came to play and to renew themselves in the strange, exhilarating climate for another spell of work down in the blazing heat of the plains, is perhaps facing a very different future. But there are many Indians and Europeans who deplore the defacement of the beautiful landscape on the outskirts of the town, where already Major Bob Jago and Chowey and the ladies would be hard put to it to recognize the country. For besides the disappearance of the open slopes that have been eaten by the enormous new factory development and, beyond that, by the latest of a chain of dams that is being built, there are other changes on the Downs. The axe has been laid to many of the giant trees that made tunnels of scented shade along the road for the walker—the giant silvery eucalyptuses and the feathery blue-green Australian wattles that had been planted from seed brought to India by the men of the old Madras Army. Ooty has moments, not only here, of recalling the last act of 'The Cherry Orchard'. Then, the Forestry Department has planted mile after mile of what used to be windswept hillside with young trees for firewood. Some of these plantations are already tall; some are so new that the infant saplings are barely visible, or bristle out of the skyline like slivers of almonds sticking out of a dish of trifle. But when they, too, wheel and deploy in armies across the hills, the character of Ooty's marvellous natural setting will be much changed. Before many years go by, the march of progress, I hear it prophesied, will probably mean the end of the hill station's social history that has been so carefully enshrined in the albums at the Club. Nowadays, only one Ooty resident still rides out of a morning on the Downs—one of the members of the regular women's bridge four—and she does not hunt any more. The present Master of the Ootacamund Hunt is a sunburned young European woman whose husband is in a British firm in Coonoor and whose picture will surely be a handsome addition to that solemn gallery of gentlemen in the Club dining room, and the meets are attended by only perhaps seven or eight loyal enthusiasts among the officers who are taking courses at the Staff College down in Wellington. Not only the attendance but the hunting country has dwindled. The industrial area and the dams and the afforestation schemes have cut up the lie of the land, so that the sportsmen must go farther and farther afield to get a run. The new plantations are helpful to the jackals, who dive into them as nimbly as a man with the police after him might leg it down into the underground, and the thickly planted young trees also serve as shadowy camouflage and corridors for panthers, to whom one of old Pilgrim's well-fed descendants is the equivalent of a toothsome *bœuf en daube*. Not so long ago, the Master told me, the pack worked through a *shola*—one of the wooded ravines between the hills—and emerged a couple of hounds short. For all these reasons, the long reign of the Horse at Ootacamund may be drawing to its close, though the Master is hopeful, she says, of the new Commandant at the Staff College, who is said to be a keen hunting man.

To see the Downs as they used to be, you have to go many miles out, bumping along the new dirt roads that have been constructed to take equipment and men to the dams. When you stop the engine of your car, there is no sound but the breeze blowing and the singing of larks. The sprinkling of tiny milky-blue and sulphur-yellow flowers in the short, springy turf might be growing above Poynings or the Devil's Dyke in Sussex, and so might the gorse bushes, which were the result of a Jove-like perambulation by a Mr. Rhode—possibly a homesick Sussex man —in 1860. He got the seed from England, filled his pockets, walked out on the Downs, and scattered it wherever the fancy took him. The Indian earth, a fertile Danaë, welcomed the visitation and reproduced the golden shower all over the place. The tangle of *sholas*, thickly grown over with flat-topped, metallic-looking dark trees and the rampaging crimson wild tree-rhododendron—a gaunt hill gypsy that seems far removed from its luscious tamed and manicured relations in Western municipal shrubberies—are pure India, and mysterious. Their silence is oppressive. Not a twig stirs in them; no patch of spotted sun and shadow moves and fades farther into the gloom. But you may be in time to see the last two or three disappearing shapes of a family of attenuated black monkeys, like a troupe of trapeze artists got up to the ears in the dishevelled shaggy fur that was modish in the twenties, who have just finished their act and are swinging grumpily away into the flies. Otherwise, there is no living soul to be seen until, going on, you come across a group of Todas sitting peacefully among the wild flowers by the side of the road while the chunky taupe buffaloes plod over the grass with their wide swimming motion, as though lifting each foot with a squelch out of a flooded paddy field. At the moment, the country is ominously dry, though; the rain gods are still in bad humour with India. Later in the year, before the longed-for monsoon begins, the Downs may be burnt and sear, but now the turf still looks fresh. The brilliant morning light lays long violet and turquoise shadows against the flanks of the Nilgiris, the Blue Hills, which can be the colour of a mountain harebell at a distance or turn, when a storm is gathering, into a jagged sketch dashed off in purple ink against a charcoal paper sky. *Nila*, 'blue'; *giri*, 'a mountain'—the name seems straightforward enough, but there is a story that it does not refer to any alchemy of light or atmosphere. The hills were given this name, according to the legend, because of the shrubby pale-blue wild flower *Strobilanthus kunthiansus*, which capriciously blooms only at intervals of from seven

74

to twelve years but then, deciding to do the thing properly, has one enormous outburst of blossom that floods over the slopes like a summer sea.

Suddenly, rounding a corner, you may come out of solitude into the bustle and chatter of one of the work camps. There are rows of corrugated godowns and a little provision shop from which people buying things look out curiously at the sound of a car. A truck clatters away over a crazy, quaking bridge into a clearing where twenty or thirty women in dark, dusty saris are squatting on the ground chipping away at big blocks of stone. The men lift the finished stones and stagger away with them. Across the valley is the half-finished wall of the new dam, with little dots of colour swarming over it—a procession of ants toting the ubiquitous round baskets that in India are used to transport anything from one place to another. If the day of the Horse has nearly finished in Ooty, the reign of the Machine has not yet entirely set in. There are concrete mixers and other large pieces of machinery standing here and there, beached high and dry in the red dust marked with patterns of bare toe prints, but the procession of ants goes on forever, and the women squat on the ground and chip away and sing. Yet if the wild, lovely place and the apparition of the Toda party placidly settled by the roadside give the onlooker the feeling that nothing much has changed here since the days of John Sullivan—or, indeed, in all the centuries that great palaces and fortresses and rulers' tombs have been getting themselves built in just this fashion—then the dam and the spreading white octopus of the film factory, the rattling trucks, the new satellite town, the girls working in the shops and offices back in Ooty, and other animated or inanimate witnesses of all kinds seem to say: No, this is different, this is change. Perhaps, at last, this may be the real change for Ootacamund.

PART FIVE

Ooty at the beginning of this century recalled to an Indian civil servant named J. Chartres Molony Guy de Maupassant's description of a village in Algeria that was inhabited solely by generals. For it seemed to Mr. Molony, strolling past the spick-and-span bungalows where a bull terrier or a couple of wirehairs would be lying on the lawn, and the *mahli* would be tying up the rambler roses, and maybe the owner himself would be making a brisk tour of inspection of the sweet peas and the begonias he intended to exhibit in next week's Flower Show, that on half the gateposts one read nothing but the names of generals or, at any rate, colonels. One had the feeling of living in the pages of an old Army List. Officers of the Indian Army often chose to retire here, in a country they loved, among people who talked their own shop, instead of going home to obscurity in a villa in Cheltenham or Bath. In a pleasant book he wrote about South India, Mr. Molony quotes some of the names of the old military families, whose sons would go as naturally and as inevitably into the Army as the day snuffs out the stars looking down on Ootacamund—names like Liardet, Penton, Tillard, Baker.

After Independence, in 1947, the British residents began to sell their houses and their belongings in Ooty and head for home. Some of those who left in the first big exodus from India but later returned have stories of the long, uncomfortable journey, packed eight in a four-berth cabin, or worse, on old passenger ships that had been converted into troopers and were often not built for service in hot climates. The Europeans who chose to stay, some of whom remain in Ooty today, have made it their last port for a variety of reasons. They are mostly the widows or daughters of men who were here in the past and stayed on after Independence, or they are retired business or government people or planters, who may have lived their working lives in other parts of India but wished to retire to deat old Ooty, the scene of so many happy times, because they are convinced there is nowhere like it in the world. Then, there are Europeans whose churches have brought them here since the war. The rector of St. Stephen's is a Cambridge man, and there are Roman Catholic fathers, and a few mission workers, and Irish nuns at the Nazareth Convent. I have been staying in Ooty for some weeks, and as far as I know, there is no general's name on any gatepost now, but there are at least two colonels retired from the Indian Army. One or two of the Anglo-Indians I meet—the phrase used to be applied in Kipling's day to the British in India, but somewhere along the line it has come to attach itself to people of mixed European and 'country', as they say here, blood—run businesses in the town. And then there are a few representatives of the really old Ooty families, such as the Misses Dot and Queenie Wapshare, descendants of the famous General Ochterlony whose statue stands in Calcutta. Members of a clan that once owned vast property in the neighbourhood, they live in Rosemount, their gently flaking old house with a noble pillared portico, which one Miss Wapshare runs as a private hotel.

I try to discover how many Europeans there are altogether in Ootacamund, but everyone supplies a different answer, and I begin to feel sympathy with Sir Frederick Price, a retired civil servant who compiled a portly 'History of Ootacamund' in 1908 for private subscribers. The difficulties of collecting his material, he says, made his task formidable—though I suspect that he loved every moment of it—for the official records of early days in the settlement had been carelessly scattered, like clues in a bureaucratic paper chase organized by fiendish tax collectors, among the dusty, bulging files of five separate government offices, and many of the documents, he found, had nourished dynasties of silver fish or had been lost or destroyed by over-efficient clerks consigning mildewed papers to the flames. When he got on the trail of old residents, they were disinclined to be communicative, or unable to be so, having died. What memories the still living Ooty dwellers produced for him were 'not always correct', as he courteously puts it, and generally the facts were difficult to check.

'About thirty families or thereabouts' is the approximate number I am most often given for the Europeans living in Ooty now, but I think that quite a few of the 'families' must consist of a solitary member, male or female. For the little family parties I do see occasionally having tea at the Ootacamund Club on a Sunday—the mothers leafing through *Vogue* while the children jig about and bounce on the sofas and waken surprised echoes in the place—have come up to Ooty, I gather, from the tea plantations or from Coonoor, twelve miles down the valley. On the day that the schools here open a new term, it is startling to find Spencer's suddenly full of little boys and girls, lively as puppies, rushing about choosing toffees and fruit drops to soften the pain of parting from their parents, who are at the counters doing the same thing by buying a bottle or two of gin and a pile of tinned stuff and fancy groceries to take home with them in the all at once horribly empty car to the far tea estate or company bungalow. But I do not meet any European children—or, indeed, any young European man or woman—who are living in Ooty.

The local children are a perpetual delight—the little girls in their ankle-length, brightly coloured skirts and short-sleeved blouses, their sleek heads sometimes banded

81

with waxy white and melon-pink flowers, and the bullet-headed, bright-eyed little boys who rush chattering along the soft red lane from the nursery school in the hollow near my hotel. The lane is a favourite short-cut, and life channels cheerfully through it. A cow wanders along, looking for a comfortable bank on which to fold herself neatly, like a collapsing opera hat, and two young men engaged in earnest discussion race, waving their hands, up the little hill towards St. Stephen's. Farther on, where the path meets another that winds vaguely off in the direction of the bazaar and the lake, a young couple are saying goodbye. Their conversation is English, their condition universal. (The infant voices I hear intoning lessons as I pass the nursery school are speaking Tamil, but the higher grades in all the municipal schools are taught in English.) 'Will you be there at six? Oh, say you will come!' 'Well, I cannot be quite certain.' Both of them certain and well pleased, they part. She flutters in her lilac *sari* down the lower track; he rushes after the arguing young men. And during the lunch hour, and after tea, there are always more young men out of the nearby offices playing a sort of badminton on a dirt court in front of the Telegraph Office, with much laughter and athletic leapings and good-humoured comment from watching friends. 'Oh, jolly good!' they cry. 'Excellent! Positively excellent shot!' In the bazaar, the cinemas display their enormous, unvarying coloured posters depicting a beautiful, doe-eyed young woman and a slightly plump but handsome man gazing tenderly into each other's glossy and elegantly arranged hair—the Indian Dream, it seems, for which the huge new octopus of a film-manufacturing plant has been built to reel out the stuff that such dreams are made of.

Like a pair of vast amorous deities—decorous modern versions of the abundantly fleshed, luscious women and tirelessly virile men in the erotic temple sculptures—they loom above the passersby and murmur of the universal condition of love and youth here as everywhere.

82

Briskly passing before these shrines, many members of the European community walk through the bazaar on a Tuesday, the great day on which they and everybody else wend their way to the market. Most of the Europeans I see there are women dressed in loose tailored suits of old-fashioned cut, a topee or beret firmly level on their heads, with a businesslike shoulder bag, perhaps, swinging by a strap. Occasionally, a man can be seen—a husband whose wife is ill or away, or maybe a bachelor—carefully prodding a papaya or buying some onions, while the market boys who tote the purchases in big, round baskets to the waiting cars for four annas stand negligently, gracefully waiting, and the liquid-eyed stallkeepers, lounging in the shade, look on impassively or exchange polite smiles when an obviously well-known lady customer, in a topee surely constructed for Edwardian elephant-hunting expeditions, trumpets, 'Give you eight annas for the lot!'

The market is beautiful, though you are told by European residents that it used to be a whole lot cleaner. (No prizes offered for guessing correctly its immaculate period.) If I lived in Ooty, I feel, there would be every reason to become a vegetarian. The meat market is an alley lined with the hung carcasses of small, horribly intact lambs, which the butchers, leaping to their feet, hack apart like energetic Herods, holding out an innocent leg and passionately inviting one to judge of its beauty, youth, and tenderness. But the Ooty vegetables are famous. Baskets of them travel down to the sweltering inhabitants of the plains every week, often passing the fish swimming up to market from the warm seas of Calicut. The vegetable market is a cornucopia of the munificent richness of the Nilgiri earth. I like to imagine Mr. Sullivan, the garden-loving Collector, walking slowly from stall to stall and eyeing with pride the mounds of small, pinkish Ooty potatoes, the snowy turnips, the rosy radishes, the big, glossy orange tomatoes, the brilliant green of the string beans, peas, artichokes, lettuce, and (as a sign that the

83

British have been here) the tiny, delicate Brussel sprouts, no bigger than a thumbnail—all washed and trimmed and arranged with art in a huge vegetable still-life.

The part of the market where the 'country' vegetables are sold is even more beautiful. Here you buy the parrot-green limes; the round, lilac-stained *brinjal*; the shiny capsicum; the pale-brown fruit of the palmyra palm, looking like baskets of lightly baked bread rolls; the gnarled bread-fruit itself; the delicious ladies' fingers that melt in the mouth in a curry; the snake vegetable, which resembles a plump, flexible cobra and coils obligingly round its purchaser's arm as he walks away; the little green wild guavas that grow in the jungle; and neat bouquets of curry leaves. All these vegetables and fruits seem to echo and be part and parcel of the colours worn by the dark, almost black-skinned women who have brought them in to market. Up here you see few of the Shocking pinks and marigold yellows and clear scarlet saris that make a zinnia border of a city street in the plains. The palette is a cooler, more sombre one, as though the Ooty frosts had nipped the dyes—raisin browns, strange greens, a sad, dark violet, tawny russets, dusty greenish mustards. Their dark-brown wearers appear to have grown out of market-garden soil, too, and to be swathed in autumnal husks, rinds, and fruit skins.

Miss Myers asks me to come with her to the market one morning to look for someone who can overhaul her typewriter. We walk by the cobblers' corner, where six or seven old men sit on the ground hammering away at piles of ancient sandals that seem to have come to rest beside them from utter weariness, and past the gleaming pots-and-pans shops and the wild-looking white-daubed fortune teller, with his cage of little parrots that will pick out a card to indicate a client's fate. Passing the handkerchiefs and the toys and the glass bangles stuck on a pointed stick like doughnuts, we come to the Modern Haircutting Saloon and to the picture stalls, where you can buy a text, 'God Is Love', or a hospitable 'Welcome', or a sad Christ of the Sacred Heart pointing at his riven breast, or a picture of Siva walking in a brilliant architectural landscape populated by scarlet and blue demons, or a St. George plunging his lance into the dragon, or a Mahatma Gandhi.

There is also, tacked up at the back of someone's stall and not for sale, a brightly coloured print representing President Kennedy striding out buoyantly beside Pandit Nehru in unclouded sunshine among flowering rhododendrons somewhere. President Kennedy has not been forgotten up here in Ooty, but the art of repairing a typewriter has, it seems. 'Typing Jobs Done,' says a hopeful notice not far from the flapping bead curtain of the Bombay Vegetarian Hotel. The owner of the shop, it turns out, will be glad to fix up the careful copying of any documents but cannot check the health of an Olivetti. 'It's difficult to get things mended in Ooty,' Miss Myers says, with resignation. 'So many of the people who used to do that sort of thing have gone.' She hoists her sunshade and goes off to buy her usual bunch of plaintains, narrowly inspecting several before she chooses the right one.

The other European ladies I see in the market are also, I notice, making their purchases with care as they walk from stall to stall, stopping to chat with friends, and sometimes speculatively eyeing the contents of each other's baskets. ('Now what on *earth* can Mona be wanting with all that sugar-cane? Well, perhaps she's buying it to give to the servants.') Food prices, I am told, are going up, having already leaped alarmingly, and there is great complaint in Ooty among the poorer townsfolk. The famous Nilgiri potatoes, for instance, used to be about seven rupees a sack; they are now seventy-five, and a hundred in the season. In this marvellously rich combined vegetable patch and dairy, eating is not the harrowing problem it is down in Kerala, where rioters have been blocking roads and smashing property in protest against the pitiful rice ration, but paying often is. Some of the ladies buy cautiously, entering the sums spent in a businesslike little book. In a community that contains a good few retired people living on pensions, the saving of rupees is nothing to be ashamed of, and the air of Ooty seems to breathe much the same gentle but firm insistence on the niceness of being not too well off and the vulgarity of being really rolling as did the air of Cranford. If mending and making do are not local virtues, they are practised ardently by many European residents who like to 'keep things nice', and do so even if their domain has shrunk to a scrupulously neat room somewhere with suitcases piled on the wardrobe and photographs on the mantelpiece of a pretty woman in a big, ospreyed hat facing a blue-eyed, whiskered man, together with more modern snapshots of a nephew's jolly kiddies playing rounders on a Surrey lawn. Restraint and economy are necessary, the 'done thing'. When I take a taxi down to Coimbatore to meet a plane, I am told that the first-class bus, really very comfortable, does the journey for a fraction of the price—'What a pity you didn't know!' I plead feebly that there was luggage to bring back on the return journey. 'The *bus* takes luggage *perfectly* well' is the pained answer. Even if some people here are better off than others, they do not parade the difference. Independence in '47, an acquaintance explains, was really a wonderful leveller in every way, like a sudden emergency at sea that dumps everyone in the same boat and lands them on an isolated island with no social pretensions and no special caste garments. The Government House set, the hunting set, the *sahibs* and the *mem-sahibs* had gone, as thoroughly as 'the peons in red livery' Mr. Molony recalled in his book, who 'sprang like mushrooms from the ground' at the start of every Ooty season. The residents who chose to remain were, simply, Europeans. 'And we're so few now that we have to hang together,' my acquaintance says. 'Any snobbery, or anything like that, is finished.'

Most of the Europeans I meet say candidly that they have decided to live in Ooty permanently, sometimes after experimenting elsewhere, principally because they think money goes further here than it does at 'home'—the real 'home', England, U.K., the strange, exasperating, damp-ridden island to which many of them have returned only on leaves since they were young there, and which they know now mainly through the newspapers in the Library and the booming voice of the B.B.C. For people with modest incomes, money does not stretch, even in Ooty, as far as it did. Rents have gone up steeply, as well as the food prices, now that industry is moving here and there is 'not a corner in Ooty to be had'—any more than there was when the British started coming up to the newly discovered Nilgiris in Sullivan's day. Some householders declare that it does not stretch at all, and that retired British Government people who receive a pension are at a particular disadvantage nowadays, since Whitehall, calculating (wrongly, they maintain) that the cost of living in India is lower than it would be in South Kensington or Cheltenham or Bath, adjusts these pensions to less than their recipients would receive if they returned to England. But however careful a watch has to be kept on expenditure, it seems to me, money is seldom so inelastic that it will not extend to a house servant and perhaps to a *mahli*-sweeper, though, again, the big new Hindustan Photo Film plant out on the Downs is stretching its arm into the town and pulling towards itself the servants, who know that they will get far better money there, and who already often prefer to work, for the same reason, in the established Government cordite factory or in another modern plant, which manufactures needles, both on the road down to Coonoor.

My acquaintances say now and then that they would like to 'go home' if it were not that, after all this time, they feel they could not stand the poky houses, the cooking, the washing up, the not having a bathroom to yourself. Even though a bathroom in the old-fashioned Ooty houses may consist of a tiled area with a drain in one corner to take the water from your hip-tub, at least it is yours; to one used to the spacious scale of these rooms, the Lyme Regis bungalow or the Bayswater flatlet doubtless seems claustrophobic. And the climate! Above all, the climate! 'I have not had a winter "at home" for many years,' says Miss Myers, pulling her chair farther back on the veranda so that the fierce early-morning sun ('as if two suns were shining instead of one,' a Victorian visitor well described it) does not burn her cheek as she types, on the ailing typewriter, the answers to her morning's mail. She does not know, she says, how she would weather one now. I meet couples who did go back to England intending to settle down, but England welcomed them sourly. Autumn came, and the cold, grubby fogs descended, and the bronchitis and the influenza moved in. Or it was 'the awful winter', when every tree became a marvellous, blinding chandelier, clanking its lustres of ice in the bitter wind, and the coal ran short, and the gas pressure and electricity were so low that you couldn't cook your chops—so here they are, back in dear old Ooty, for where in the world (such sagas are bound to end) could you hope to find a better climate? Taking account of all its drawbacks— the isolation, the shortage of entertainment and of new faces, the loneliness—they love the place. Many of the Europeans have good friends among the Indian residents who also love Ooty and live here all the year round, and time goes by pleasantly, on the whole. Time itself, after all, is a democratic leveller, and if there is nobody very young in Ooty any more, the community does not seem to notice it except by making a few wry jokes about itself now and then. The situation brings its own compensations, like an unexpectedly thoughtful present. 'I'm not really sorry it's over,' one woman says when describing to me— in her amusing throaty, hoarse 'period' voice, which makes me think of the twenties and green hats and Tallulah— Ooty's gay days of parties and gymkhanas and big balls at the different princes' 'palaces' up on Rajah's Square. 'After all, I wouldn't be interested in balls now.' Lovely Ooty, faithfully growing older, too, has put away her own ball dress, and the music has finished.

I meet an agreeable ex-Indian Army colonel, a bachelor, who is one of the residents who gave U.K. a try and did not care for the experiment. He has lived in India for many years. After Independence, the government asked him to stay on to help train the new Indian Army. He had been up to Oooty several times and had liked it so well that when his retirement finally came he bought a house here. 'It was different then,' he says. 'There were many more friends in those days, and I kept a horse and rode on the Downs every morning. I played golf, and there was plenty to do. It was really a very pleasant life.' Then he decided to throw everything up and go back to England, where he has several relatives. But it was the old story of finding London preoccupied, rackety, much changed, and expensive; living at his club or in one of those dim hotels peopled by retired Army men and elderly ladies were the possible alternatives, and he could not face them. He came back to Ooty. His erect figure in its tweed suit, woolly pullover, and neat bow tie might have marched in from the Parade at Cheltenham. He serves on the Library Committee and is a sidesman at St. Stephen's, and the old butler at Willingdon House says 'Salaam, Colonel Sahib' when they meet— a conditioned reflex. Ooty, too, he found, had changed while his back was turned. Many of the old faces had gone, the town was swarming with people, and prices were rising alarmingly. The colonel had got rid of his house here when he went to England, and all he could find now was half a house, owned by an Indian landlord, which he occupies somewhat uneasily. The tenant of the other half is a Hindu holy man—a *saddhu*. 'Very nice, quiet chap, very polite, asked me to go for a walk the other day,' the colonel tells me. 'He hardly speaks any English, but I felt I had to say yes.' So off paced the tweed suit and the saffron robe, amiably conjoined for a silent stroll. All the same, the colonel would like to move, he admits, if he could find somewhere to go. He spends his time house-hunting, but he can find nothing that is not too steep for the means of a retired Army man. Once again, it seems, he is toying with the thought of England, though that practically mythical place, when it is invoked by the exiles here, seems to have much in common with a woman who looms larger and infinitely more desirable in a man's thoughts when she is far away, but would probably disappoint him if she turned up across the breakfast table every morning. The colonel cross-questions me about the cost of living at home in U.K. What is the price of a pound of butter, for instance? 'There you are! It's dearer in Ooty!' he cries triumphantly. Even though one cannot live on butter alone, the colonel might be tempted to try his luck again—for I think he is lonely here—if it were not for one reason that prevents him. He has an Indian servant to whom he is devoted and who is stricken with a serious illness that must eventually prove fatal. The colonel will not leave (if he ever does) while his servant is alive. One day, perhaps, he can settle the man's wife and children comfortably and then depart. It is his tie of the affections, and it binds him to India.

One hears unenvious stories of the people who have gone back to England and, hardier or luckier, have adapted themselves to the new life—of the old lady, past eighty, who took along, as though determined that India should go with her, the kitchen grinding stone on which to pound the spices and chilis for her daily curry; of couples who bought houses near old friends from Madras or Bombay but, after all, found themselves unable to 'settle', and winged restlessly off again, like swallows drawn back to a nest above a sunbaked wall, to try some kinder island in a warm blue sea. All the same, academic discussions of maybe one day returning to England, even though the Socialists are in power and everything must be so different, are to be heard not infrequently in Ooty, rather as the

A CHILDREN'S PARTY AT THE MAHARAJAH OF JODHPUR'S SUMMER RESIDENCE, ARANMORE, OOTY, 1935

Reproduced by kind permission of Miss Beatrix Blake

THE MOUNTAIN RAILWAY, OOTY

D.I.P., Madras

three sisters spoke of going to Moscow. I hear the pros and cons run over, perhaps not too seriously, by acquaintances who I somehow doubt will ever turn the nostalgic talk into an airline ticket except to go back on a visit—and even that is impossible now for those who do not have money waiting for them in English accounts somewhere, or else hospitable relatives or friends with 'Welcome' displayed on their doors as large as it hangs in the picture stall in the market. The Government of India forbids Europeans (as it does its own nationals) to take rupees out of the country except for studying some approved subject in a foreign university or for doing business that will bring foreign currency back into India. If I feel sometimes that Ooty is a bit claustrophobic itself, enclosed like a goldfish bowl in the circle of hills looking down into it like big cats, that feeling is shared, it seems, by Indians I meet who shrug their shoulders and say that 'until India is strong' it is necessary. 'I think it will be perhaps ten years before we can feel that our Amy is so strong that we are secure from China and Pakistan,' a young civil servant says. 'I have a brother who is a doctor in Birmingham, and I should like to visit him. But we have to put all such ideas out of our minds at the moment, of course.' Many Europeans I meet, though, have managed to take a trip home quite recently by one means or another, and even those who perhaps have no hope or intention of doing so like to talk of England, of London, on a note of amiable tolerance, as of some dear, doubtless much altered old friend whom they have not seen for years but would not dream of dropping because she is not the girl she used to be. The Army and Navy Stores, the In-and-Out Club, the London Pavilion, and a fearfully good little restaurant in Frith Street that used to give remarkable three-and-six-penny lunches before the war are likely to crop up in conversations. 'Where exactly is that in Bond Street? On the right or left as you go up from Piccadilly?' a voice floats across the dining-room of the Club at lunchtime, and

91

Ooty's afternoon grows dim as the red buses thunder by outside the windows, where the heliotrope growing in tall hedges of pale-purple chenille turns for a moment, to the reflective eye, into sooty railings. Even by such frail threads, it is good to be able to feel that one can find one's way back.

The only people in Ooty—outside the European community, that is—who occasionally express nostalgia for the days of the British are, naturally, people in lines of business that catered for them, and old servants who sometimes remember them with affection. There is no town in all India that was sorrier to see them go than Ooty, says a stout taxi-driver, looking nonchalantly over his shoulder at me as he makes a terrifying series of swerves towards a sheer drop below the roadside. I am stopped in the street by an effusive elderly woman with a diamond stud in her nose who cries, clasping my arm, that I must surely be sister to a, I think, Mrs. Seth-Martingale, a very lovely lady who used to live in Ooty, generous and beloved by all. 'I went to her house for years to sew,' she says. The old butler at Willingdon House worked for a major's family and sighs like a melancholy ancient spaniel as he recalls it, standing thin and bowed in his green tunic coat. 'Ah, those were the happy days—yes, very happy days. Now poor India has no luck at all.' And when I go to have my hair done at the little hairdresser's shop—the grandly named Royal Saloon, which lurks down some steps opposite the Nilgiri Library—I hear the same plaints.

The Royal is a tiny, cluttered place without windows, every inch of its walls covered with bright pictures and tacked-up postcards and clippings—comic animals dressed as golfers; lovely, haughty girls from a hair-styles paper; a calendar of a chubby child in a pink loincloth chasing a butterfly towards a pool covered with blue lotus flowers and being plucked back from watery death by a sagacious, limpid-eyed dog; an Edwardian photograph of a puppy having its paw bandaged by a London bobby kneeling to the job while its owner, a ragged urchin, looks on, and the Law tells the patient soothingly, 'All right, ol' chap, we won't 'urt you.' The Royal's effect is soothing, too—a sort of drowsy, sheltered return to the womb combined with the nursery, for the shampoo and drying operations are done by hand. I bow obediently over the basin while brass ewers of warm water are sloshed over my head. Careful as a nannie, the proprietor, a serious-looking grey-haired man, stands delicately moving the hand dryer, later, up and down. He is the only hairdresser left in Ooty to whom the ladies come, yet I can see as he opens his appointment book that the day's entries do not exactly crowd one another. And business has been getting worse, he affirms, ever since more British left. 'But the Indian ladies?' Indian ladies do not have hair; that is, qualifying the startling statement, they have far too much hair—long, magnificent tresses that most of them prefer to wash and arrange at home and otherwise leave alone. The only hair he recognizes as hair, I infer, is pliable stuff in which the razor can have a field day, artistically thinning and shaping it into one of the cute styles portrayed on the wall. Regarding them sadly, as a man shut out forever from paradise might yearn through the bars at the peris, the proprietor adds, after a moment's thought, 'One Parsi family, the daughters having short hair.' Several of the European ladies come to him, of course, and one or two who return to England for visits bring him back hair lacquer and rollers and other things hard or expensive to get in Ooty. But he is feeling the pinch, and so are several other businesses in Ooty that used to do well on hill-station visitors' trade.

Looking through an old British magazine he hands me, I wonder why I am reminded of something I read the other day, and suddenly I remember what it was. In the Library, I came across a little pamphlet published in the eighteen-fifties containing the private reports of the Residents in several parts of India that had previously been ruled by native princes. The Residents had been asked to give their opinion on how the local inhabitants were settling down under British law and order after the old tyrannous régimes, and at least one reported bluntly that in his district the people did not like the change at all but bitterly regretted the princely days. The vast splendour kept up by the ruler had provided jobs for everyone, and the air was filled with the lamentations of out-of-work goldsmiths, jewellers, silk and carpet merchants, musicians, singers, tailors, perfume and sweetmeat sellers, conjurers, dwarfs, elephant mahouts, astrologers, servants, and dancers, to whom a few British and their starchy *mem-sahibs* were no consolation.

The Friend in Need Society exists to succour the old grooms and gardeners and ayahs who were marooned in Ooty when the British tide went out in its turn, and occasionally a stranded European, too—for 'There are some old residents here who are living on the smell of an oily rag,' as someone puts it with awful clarity. They are people who stayed on in Ooty after Independence because they had nowhere else to go and would not have cared to leave anyway—widows without families to look after them, whose husbands had perhaps retired to Ooty and left them a little money, which one day suddenly became no money at all, or daughters of old residents who are now alone, poor, and ageing themselves, or old men whose relatives in England have forgotten them except for an occasional Christmas letter. These are the sad little shipwrecks of history who were beached and would have been left to rust if it were not for another observation post that is quietly trained on Ooty and every other part of India where British people are still living. The United Kingdom Citizens Association has its headquarters in Calcutta and branches in most of the big cities. It keeps an eye on British interests everywhere, and sometimes helps someone to go back to England, or provides a modest port in a storm and a tiny monthly pension for ladies who might otherwise, in genteel Cranford fashion, starve quietly to death, their trim buckled belts pulled in and every hair on their heads in place, for things would be 'kept nice', one feels sure, up to the end.

There are public-spirited Europeans in Ooty who concern themselves with these societies a good deal and with other, more broadly based projects having to do with civic good. They are the ones who sit also on the committees of the Library and the Culture Centre and are interested in their church or in one or another of the several excellent schools that flourish here—the successors of a boys' school, now defunct, that was started by a Reverend Mr. Rigg in the eighteen-forties, and of an also long-vanished Establishment for Young Ladies, opened at about the same time by a Miss Hale and her two nieces, where the little Amelias and Beckys were requested to arrive with their own cots and bedding and a silver fork and spoon apiece. All in all, there is a good deal going on that reminds me of life in an English village, not least because the names of the same members of the community are apt, I notice, to show up in all the activities. I am told that there are several energetic Parsi members of the various groups, but not many Indian residents, it seems, show much desire to take the lead or to sit on committees. 'It is generally we Europeans who do most of the donkey work,' one man grumbles mildly to me. 'And after *we* go—for none of us, after all, are exactly chickens—who is going to carry on with the jobs, I wonder? I suppose all these things will simply fade quietly away when we do.'

Miss Myers takes me one Friday evening to a meeting of the Culture Centre at the Indian Union Club—a long, low, pleasantly shabby bungalow that seems to sigh and rustle to itself a good deal as it looks out into a tangled garden. The members arrive by ones and twos, strolling up the drive and standing chatting for a few minutes on the veranda. It is a small turnout tonight, Miss Myers explains, for it is one of the occasional musical evenings instead of a lecture. Next week, for instance, a young local lawyer is booked to talk on 'Common Sense and the Law', and the indefatigable Sir C. P. Ramaswami Aiyar is listed in the programme of future speakers on the topic 'Is Religion Necessary?' But tonight our programme is to be gramophone records chosen by Mr. Hazari, a grey-haired, amiable Anglo-Indian who has a photographer's business in the town and whose family has long and firm ties with Ooty. Music, it seems, is less of a draw, particularly for the Indian members, who often find Western composers difficult.

This evening, out of the little band of nine music lovers who eventually assemble, there are only two Indians present—the willowy wife of another lawyer, who tells me enthusiastically that she would not care to live anywhere else in India, and the lady who works in the Library and who has added a gay pink flower to her hair for the occasion. Then there is a tall, thin Dutchman with a merry eye, and a girl from one of the missions who is up here to learn Tamil, and a small blonde woman who has the movements of a bird and perches on one of the shabby sofas under a big photograph of Pandit Nehru, cocking her head towards the gramophone as though anticipating crumbs. She is an artist, Miss Myers tells me later, whose family used to live in Ooty; now she lives alone at one of the hotels. 'I remember her years ago at a fancy-dress ball at the Club,' Miss Myers says. 'She was dressed as a mermaid—lovely skin she had, and her hair all hanging down. Quite a picture!'

The cultural circle is completed by the headmistress of St. Hilda's School for Girls and Miss Queenie Wapshare, in tweeds, her waved grey hair smartly blue-rinsed, who has walked over from nearby Rosemount and sits down in a back row of the lines of chairs. The high-ceilinged room, built on the old Ooty pattern, must be always rather dim anyway, but the twilight is deepened by partly drawn curtains.

'We are going to begin with Mozart's Haffner Symphony, conducted by Otto Klemperer,' says Mr. Hazari. He starts the record player and sits down. The strong, gay, confident voice rings out through the room, stating 'I am here' as simply as all those serious hunting men who line the Ooty Club dining-room walls in photographs say it in their different ways as they stare into the sunshine from the backs of their big horses, taking India and their place in the saddle superbly for granted. The young woman from the mission leans back, folds her arms across her jumper, and closes her eyes. The mermaid-bird lifts her narrow face and appears to half float, half fly in some buoyant element of pleasure. Some of the listeners gaze down, some stare abstractedly at Mr. Nehru or at a faded patch on the walls. Miss Myers reads the sleeve of the record judiciously, then leans over and passes it on to a neighbour, as if it were the chart circulated from the captain of our plane, giving details of the flight and advising us to look out of the window to catch the beauty of the *Andante* unfolding from the mist and to fasten our seat belts for the *Prestissimo*. Mr. Hazari is fond of Mozart. We have the first two movements of the Clarinet Concerto, played by Bernard Watson and the Philharmonia Orchestra, conducted by Herbert Von Karajan. 'Now I thought you would enjoy a little ballet music by Delibes,' Mr. Hazari announces. After 'Sylvia', for whom we do not fly so far, though the lawyer's wife taps her foot and the little artist sways to the beat as though she might whirl into the dance at any minute, there is an intermission while a servant goes round with a tray of coffee. We end the evening on a lighter cultural level with 'The Pirates of Penzance' and a *pot-pourri* of popular old songs. 'Over the seas to Skye', hums the headmistress, executing a few gliding dance steps as she crosses the room to talk to Miss Myers, and the artist asks plaintively if we cannot have 'My Fair Lady'. 'Freda, you *always* want "My Fair Lady".'

'It is a pity, really, that it was a music night,' says Miss

Myers as we walk home. It is absolutely dark now, for twilight in Ooty comes with an abrupt clap that can almost be heard extinguishing things. The pure Matisse colour of the great scarlet geraniums hanging over someone's veranda has been turned off suddenly into gorgeous gloom. The air smells of something aromatic and sweet, with a whiff of a bonfire burning somewhere. Miss Myers has her flashlight and carries a light, whippy walking stick, which, though she does not say so, I think may have something to do with the tales I hear of two or three recent attacks made on women walking alone. Bad men coming into the town from outside Ooty to find work, the old butler at Willingdon House tells me. Bags have been snatched, sometimes in broad daylight, and a European lady visitor is said to have been knocked on the head after she had visited the bank to cash some travellers' checks. Bad characters, *not* Ooty people, says the old butler, coming punctiliously to collect me from my room every night for dinner, locking the door, and hiding the key swiftly in a pot of maidenhair fern, where I usually cannot find it, either.

'I wish Sir C. P. had been talking tonight,' said Miss Myers, striding briskly along the road. 'When he is giving a talk, every member turns up. That room is always absolutely packed out.'

PART SIX

O N E day, Miss Guthrie invites me to lunch to meet Sir C. P. Ramaswami Aiyar. He often visits Miss Guthrie, an old friend. When the wheels of his car crunch on the gravel, and the chauffeur, very smart in a dashingly folded puggaree, jumps out and runs round to open the door, and the old butler, salaaming, hurries to welcome him, it seems almost like a royal progress. Today, Sir C. P., as everyone calls him (*Who's Who*, when I consulted it in the Library, did not list his first names), wears a long grey coat tunic and a little round cap instead of the pepper-and-salt tweed suit he wore when he was here last, and he is accompanied by a pretty young granddaughter who has come to live with him and is just about to start a job teaching domestic science at the Nazareth Convent.

He is a charming old man of eighty-seven whose bright, twinkling eyes and incisive manner make him seem far younger than that as he talks about visits to London, where he may stay at the Athenaeum or the National Liberal Club* (though he, too, gently complains that one has to 'sling one's towel over one's shoulder, an awful bore, and walk half a mile or so to the bathroom' in these august but old-fashioned establishments), and about Lloyd George and Asquith and the prodigious F. E. Smith, whom he admired

---

* It was at the National Liberal Club that Sir C. P. Ramaswami Aiyar, K.C.S.I., K.C.I.E., died in September 1966, while on a visit that was to have included lecturing at Cambridge.

equally for his dazzling forensic powers and his ability to use them unimpaired by a large intake of brandy. Sir C. P. is busy at the moment on a book describing his own political years. Among other works, he has written a life of Mrs. Annie Besant, the Theosophist leader and thorn in the Government of India's flesh, who spent some time in enforced political cold storage at Ootacamund in a house above St. Stephen's Church.

Sir C. P. is Ooty's big man, who is deeply in everything and known with respect by everybody in the place. On Republic Day, when the flag is run up with a little cere-mony, it is he who gives the address. He is an eminent lawyer who held various high offices in the Government before Independence, and he has represented India at Geneva and elsewhere. He has been Prime Minister of Travancore, Vice-Chancellor of Travancore University and, in the fifties, of Annamalai University. His deep affection for Ooty began when he used to accompany the Madras Government on its move up here for six months of the year—April to October. He has seen many parts of the world, he says, but none to beat Ooty as a place to live, though he, too, talks rather sadly of the changes out on the Downs and of the floating labour force that is being attracted here by the new projects. He thinks that in time the old hill station will be as completely transformed as (taking for example a place he loves) the character of the city of Oxford was changed by the arrival of the Nuffield motor industry. The house he built here in the nineteen-thirties has an ornamental hedge trimmed in the shape of a procession of topiary elephants marching along with their trunks in the air, and it is an airy, spacious place, contain-ing all the acquisitions of a life of travel: ancient Mogul and Chinese paintings, pictures by modern Indian artists, Tibetan temple embroideries, Japanese porcelain, ivory Kwan-yins, very many books, and a sort of enormous dentist's chair upholstered in plush—an English contrap-tion calling itself Carter's Nest for Rest, out of which, instead of instrument tables and drilling apparatus, sprout a book rest and reading lamp and attachments to hold the studious nestling's tray or glass. When I go to visit him a few days after Miss Guthrie's lunch and am shown these things, I notice another fitting, which I suppose is connected with the old butler's 'bad characters' among the new floating population coming up to Ooty. The house seems very peaceful. A secretary sits typing in the entrance hall and servants flit about the spick-and-span compound, but tall sliding steel gates can be drawn across the staircase, so that the whole of the upper story is shut off in a virtually thief-proof cage.

Another morning, Sir C. P. having arranged that I should be allowed to go through it, I drive up to Government House, sent by him in his car behind the puggaree, which the sentries at the gate recognize instantly and wave onward up the avenue. The big, cream-coloured mansion was built in 1877 when the Duke of Buckingham was Governor of Madras. He had the pillared portico copied from Stowe, his family seat in Buckinghamshire, and the homesick ducal souvenir, sitting among its lawns, turns a large, blank face towards England. It towers over the original Government House, which had become too small to cope with growing Ooty. This still stands a little below and almost adjoining it—a modest building of cottage-like proportions and much more charm, which was used, when the British were here, to house the Governor's Military Secretary and the A.D.C.'s. The slope on which it is situated was part of the Botanical Gardens, laid out by a Mr. MacIvor, who had been sent for from Kew in 1848. He found, he says, probably with some dismay, that the upper part of the proposed gardens was 'a forest with heavy trees growing on steep and rugged banks', while the lower part was a dismal swamp 'traversed with deep ravines'. Nothing daunted, MacIvor had the forest felled and the swamp drained, and brought in exotic trees and shrubs from many other parts of the East and from Europe.

He planted Ooty's first mulberry tree, imported vines from Shiraz, and introduced the red and white camellias that still bloom—or their buxom grandchildren do—on the heights above the bandstand, which in the old days was the centre of social promenades and gossip when the Governor was in residence. I have enjoyed, on various walks in the gardens, filling the empty bandstand with the resplendent scarlet figures of the Governor's Band playing 'Soldiers of the Queen', and fancying the parasols and the huge, flowery hats and the whispering embroidered-muslin dresses of the women on the grassy slopes where now, near a proud floral map of India, I see a circle of small children sitting closs-legged in their bright clothes, chirping away like birds, waiting to catch the oranges their teacher begins throwing to them out of a red string bag. This is where, in the season, huge crowds turn out for the famous Flower Show. In Victorian days, the events used to include a competing procession of 'tastefully decorated infantile carriages', won in 1898 (as a bound volume of *Indian Gardening* in the library has imparted to me with the usual British delicacy of language about Indians) by a 'little Miss Somers-Eve', who 'sat in state in her *palki* carried by six little black boys, a tiny canopy over the little one's head with her initial "V" in violets'. The judges gave the second prize to a spanking miniature pony phaeton driven by two small sailor boys, 'the Union Jack flying merrily over their heads', who doubtless lived to see themselves and the flag and little Miss Somers-Eve reclining under her violets all bowled smartly out of the Indian scene forever.

Government House is untenanted now, and used only during the season for official entertaining. (The Governor at the time of my visit, the Maharajah of Mysore, preferred to stay in his own 'palace' when he came to Ooty.) When I have been met by the caretaker and shown into the hall, I find a subdued bustle of spring cleaning going on—rugs rolled back, men up ladders washing chandeliers, women polishing the fine teak panelling in the dining-room, where we start the tour of the state rooms. They seem to echo with more than our footsteps as we walk through, the caretaker conscientiously doing the honours of the portraits of the Governors and their ladies, whose eyes follow us, gazing out of their frames with that air of anticipation that inanimate objects in Ooty seem often to wear. I lose track of all the introductions. The men stand resplendent—gorgeous armadillos in their jackets crusted stiffly with overlapping plates of gold lace, their Court knee breeches, and rainbow chestfuls of ribbons and orders. The ladies, in full fig of stiff satins and jewels, often have sensible, motherly faces somewhat at odds with all the warm-looking finery, but I see one young woman, a romantic oval pastel portrait, who holds against her knee a small, pale girl—a perfect little languid Miss Somers-Eve. Nobody in Ooty, sensibly, has excommunicated the mementoes of British rule as, in other parts of India, the old statues have been banished from their plinths, for in a ballroom like a white-and-gold wedding cake there glooms the mourning guest at the feast—Queen Victoria, here in sable velvet and lace and the glummest of glum widow-woman expressions, posed by the artist with unconscious symbolism against a sullen sunset sky, though the sunset of Empire did not come for half a century or so after the portrait was painted. And here, too, are huge portraits of George V and George VI, robed and crowned; and Queen Mary, her golden hair dressed in a puff of tight ringlets above her pink-and-white face like a plump woven cushion on which someone has lightly laid the little coronet; and the Duke of Buckingham, a stocky, bearded party who might pass for a prosperous shopkeeper as painted by an Indian artist of the day; and more Governors and ladies in profusion. Pointing to a picture of the Royal Family group at the Westminster Abbey service for George V's Silver Jubilee, the caretaker wishes me not to miss 'present Queen and Margaret Rose as little ones'. But change is here, all the same. Over the mantelpiece, in the place of honour, startlingly underdressed and frail-looking in this gallery of well-nourished bodies in yards of sumptuous dress goods, hangs a full-length, brightly coloured modern portrait of Gandhiji. He is strolling along against a sunny landscape, benevolently smiling, a skinny figure in his dhoti, with a large turnip watch, such as an old farmer might carry, dangling from his waist. The vitality of this endearing apparition is so great that he makes all the others look slightly lifeless in their splendid clothes.

After I have been shown the A.D.C.'s sitting-room, hung with those inevitable British sporting prints of pink coats and splashed horses sailing over or coming down in water jumps, and a ladies' boudoir waiting rather pathetically for someone to arrive and dash off a chit at the pretty little white-painted writing table, we enter some other large apartment, the use of which I forget to inquire in my interest over what is happening outside the windows. For the fine, clear panes are darkened by what appears to be a thick dust storm whirling in the pillared portico. The caretaker politely introduces it, too. Rock bees—millions and millions of them, hanging in great, heaving stalactites from the portico roof and from the window frames, obscuring the sunshine with their furious dance, their thick, angry communal voice sounding loud and rather alarming, like the roar of a mob, even through the glass. The caretaker explains gravely that before His Excellency arrives and the functions begin, these formidable colonists will have been removed. But now, aside from Mr. Gandhi walking in on his thin legs and annihilating all the ladies and gentlemen in sight, they seem the only life in this official slab of a residence where at the moment nobody resides, where the past can be felt, not richly, as one feels it in the records of the Library, or belting along at a gallop, as in the Ooty Club photograph albums, but with a dead weight of vanished pomp and circumstance. 'I mind dreadfully our loss of greatness, you know,' one of the remaining British observed unexpectedly to me not long ago, and here the trappings of greatness are indeed rather melancholy, as though congealed under glass in a museum where most of the time people do not come. As instinctively as they might take possession of a rock chamber in the cliff galleries of a vanished dynasty, the bees have moved in.

Another day, still on the track of the really high life as it used to be lived in Ooty, I go to take a look at the neighbourhood of Rajah's Square, where some of the princes' 'palaces' were built, including that of Highness Mysore, as Miss Guthrie refers to the Governor. It lies beyond Mr. Sullivan's much altered lake, which quickly deteriorated after his time into a dump for garbage and filth of all kinds, though the townsfolk were still drinking the water up to 1851. As late as 1860, a Collector was airily replying, in answer to indignant criticisms of its stench and the danger to public health, that 'The sewage of London, centre of wealth and civilization, is still turned into the Thames, as that of Ooty into the lake'—so what was good enough for London, he implied, was certainly permissable for Ooty where, to be sure, the cholera arrived in 1877 and killed nearly five hundred people. Much later, they cut down the willows along the shady stretch of Willow Bund and filled in one end of the lake to make the Race Course, and today it is a pretty place where people boat and fish and take a stroll in the short evening light.

Rajah's Square, I feel, is no place for humble pedestrian exercise. It is a grandiose open space—a miniature place of occasion, surrounded by tall painted pillars supporting clusters of globular electric lamps, that looks as though it might have been designed by someone having a shot at scaling down the regal sweep outside Buckingham Palace. The layout demands imperatively an open landau containing a personage glimpsed through a stiffly trotting escort with lances at the ready, or, at the very lowest possible denomination, a fleet of discreet pearly-grey Rolls-Royces, from one of which might flash in passing a splendid blink of emeralds pinned to a sari. Whatever the Square may have seen in the past, today, when I visit it, it is full only of sunlit emptiness and a great deal of nature at its most beautiful, for nowhere else do the trees soar more nobly to lace themselves in green Gothic aisles overhead, or the lawns—nature charmingly tamed for the rich—more carefully match themselves up to emeralds than in this exclusive neighbourhood of self-consciously grand entrance gates, through which one gets glimpses of well-watered parterres. None of the weeds that the English brought with them to their new Nilgiri paradise very early on— the docks and dandelions and thistles that faithfully travelled to Ooty after them in the sacks of agricultural seeds from home—would dare to spring up here, one is certain. But I am disappointed by what I can make out of the princely 'palaces', since I had hoped for something truly Indian and exotic, instead of which these large mansions have from afar a comfortable English air, providing a flash of gables and hints of white-balustraded balconies and garden seats and glassed-in nooks that would not be out of place among the pines and rhododendrons of Ascot.

People have told me of the old days of princely entertaining in Ooty, when the catering for a ball or a reception might be ordered from some famous firm in distant Calcutta, to give added chic to the occasion. Then the entourage of such an establishment would certainly include numerous relatives and hangers-on, and the big families of children were likely to have an English comptroller to direct the education of the young princes, and a Scottish governess and a nannie, uprooted in her grey coat and round felt hat straight out of Hyde Park, as well as ayahs for the infants. And I like to imagine, as I stroll around here, one of these gateways guarded by impassive sentries in towering turbans, their big hands industriously clicking away at knitting stockings and mufflers, as they were

108

taught to do, I am told, after the Englishwoman who supervised that particular prince's young household had complained that the sight of their idleness was an unedifying example. The maharajahs who come up now for the best months of the year live less showily, and at least one of the 'palaces' in another part of Ooty, Aranmore, once the property of the Maharajah of Jodhpur, belongs to the Government today and, patriotically re-christened Tamilnagam, is used to house V.I.P.'s and for conferences. A little while ago I met on the road a group of young people hiking along, the girls in slacks and sweaters, the young men, in their tweed sports jackets, twirling walking sticks cheerfully, who came out of the gates of Tamilnagam and may have been junior government employees attending one of these conferences. Rajah's Square and the other houses of the rich have not yet become museums, but their mode of life, perhaps, is changing.

Though the Governor is 'at home' to Ooty with garden parties during the season, the days of the really lavish entertainments must surely be over. I think the social scene for most of the year is probably more like what it was in the hill station's first period, when languid, yellow-complexioned invalids were sent here to enjoy such simple pleasures as eating mutton with 'a flavour you did not recollect in India', as Richard Burton, the explorer, then a young officer in the 18th Regiment of Native Infantry, wrote in 1847, or throwing yourself on a grass bank and going into sentimental raptures over picking 'the first daisy you ever saw out of England'. It was as quiet a place then as, out of season, it is today. The convalescents walked, rode, took afternoon naps, and went to bed early, as though in some Britannic-style spa, a Nilgiri Harrogate or Droitwich where the régime was strict, and some of the Madras and Bombay ladies may have found the going rather slow. Even Dr. R. Baikie, that fervent Ooty propagandist, writes regretfully in his 1834 guidebook that 'females are sometimes less favourably impressed with the climate than those of the other sex', suffering doubtless from 'the moral effect of a quiet secluded life, as contrasted with the brilliant though heartless society they are accustomed to at most of the large stations in India'. The charms of mutton and daisies quickly palled on Burton, it is clear. In his early travel book *Goa and the Blue Mountains*, he is quite venomous in his descriptions of the rather homely entertainment that Ooty could offer a visiting subaltern on sick leave thirteen years after Baikie: the picnics and excursions and jolly Terpsichorean clumpings on the turf of some sylvan spot; the occasional *soirées* where Lieutenant Burton was expected—unfortified, as he notes bitterly, by liquor or tobacco—to hand round cakes, muffins, and scandal (then, as now, a favourite Ooty commodity) to elderly ladies; the still rarer balls, at which three scraping fiddles and a piano provided the music, the champagne was apt to be frightful 'gooseberry' stuff that gave you a terrible head in the morning, and the 'wall-flowers', a blossom generally unknown in India, were luxuriant. Then there were the endless walks round the lake and the flirting and the rides with Miss A—— to try and fill up the days somehow, and the guffawing horseplay in the smoking-room after the ladies had mercifully retired for the night. When he decided to relieve the rustic boredom by practising his Hindustani with a local teacher, he found that his mind would not work in a cold room, a dark house (he compares the architecture of Ooty bungalows rudely with that of cow houses), and 'air so exciting that it is all but impossible to sit down quietly for an hour'. At last, to his joy, he was pronounced fit to rejoin his regiment in Bombay. Fitting his toe in the stirrup and casting 'one last scowl upon Ootacamund', Burton said a blistering adieu to the spot where, in his opinion, 'a man who in other places drinks a little too freely, here seldom fails to bring on an attack of delirium tremens'. Off he rode eagerly towards his ultimate destination of Mecca and the great lakes of Central Africa. Sir Frederick Price gives a cold mention or two to Burton and his derisive criticisms in *A History of Ootacamund*, but it is plain that he cannot forgive him.

There is no word in Sir Frederick's pages, oddly enough, of another keenly observant but far more lovable visitor who did not really take to Ooty, either. On my walks, I often think of Edward Lear turning up here, a bulky, untidily dressed figure meticulously noting down for his journal the exact sounds chanted by the grunting bearers who carried him up the road in his *tonjon*, followed by his faithful Corfu servant, Georgio Kokalki, sitting in another. According to Dr. Baikie, the male leg-wear recommended for Victorian travellers to Ooty was like something out of the *Book of Nonsense*. Were Mr. Lear's own stout calves protected by a pair of patented anti-gropelos—thick anti-snake gaiters, further fortified by flat iron plates up the shinbones, that rose above the knees and could be ordered from a particular bootmaker in Calcutta? He was sixty-two, naturally timid, suffering from a bad heart, and in need of protection. Hating noise, dirt, dogs, gossiping hotel acquaintances, and the mechanics of travel, he was drawing towards the end of fourteen gruelling months in India that had exposed him to all these discomforts and more. Often his depression was so acute ('O! beastly row! O! hateful Indian travel!' he groans in his journal) that he was tempted to cut his journey short and creep home to San Remo, but then something good always caught his eye ('Roads of such redundant beauty one could hardly dream of! India, Indianissimo!'), and his cheerful spirits rose again. The visit was at the invitation of his beloved friend Thomas George Baring, 'an extremely luminous and amiable brick', as Lear described him after their first meeting in Rome, in 1847. He and Baring, a talented amateur artist, had taken to each other at once. Going off on excursions together into the Campagna, they worked happily away on

111

sketching stools planted side by side. Now, twenty-six years later, the luminous and amiable brick had put away his portfolio, made a dazzling change of clothes, and become the Earl of Northbrook and Viceroy of India. Amiable as ever and able to play the generous patron to his friend, he had suggested that Lear should visit him and travel for a year or so wherever he liked. The Viceroy would pay all expenses and was to receive in return one or two large Indian landscape paintings, to be worked up by Lear from his sketches after he returned home.

Lear turned up in Ootacamund on his tour of the south because he had been told by everybody that it was 'one of the Indian *sine qua nons'*. He stopped at a Coonoor hotel on the way, dining with a Colonel Brown who had achieved the feat, he noted, of living six years at Trichinopoly without once bothering to see the famous temples, and also with 'a coffee or tea-planting cove who talked principally of dogs' and has many a replica in the neighbourhood today, one fancies. Then, while he and Georgio were eating their picnic lunch, it came on to rain in torrents, and, a worse misfortune, he kicked the claret bottle over as he ran for shelter. 'O that it were possible to drink less!' he sighs somewhere in his journal, but it was not possible. He was able to bear the heat, the bad roads, the lean, barking dogs, the beds and sketching stools that broke under him, the crowds who followed him round to watch him draw, only with the help of the quantities of claret, brandy, beer, champagne, and sherry methodically noted in his daily entries.

But when he had struggled up to Oooty he was disappointed with the scenery. The 'odious' stony tracks jolted him hideously, the altitude upset his heart, and the reminders of home that so oddly met his eyes at every turn were not inspiring. He noted the English gorse on the Downs and the English roses round the neat little houses, and he observed that the gentle aquatints of the lake might easily be in Cumberland or Westmorland. It was hard to remember that he was still in India, Indianissimo. All was 'so English as to be, I think, utterly undrawable', he wrote, though good old Georgio, the most devoted of Sancho Panzas, did haul his master up a hill to see a vast view of the drop down to the plains—'a world of opal beaten out with a filmy horizon of light'—and seven apes looked out from the tree ferns of a dark wood at Mr. Lear as he and Georgio retraced their footsteps to Ooty. And he made a charming, airy watercolour sketch of the pearly lake and the soft green hills under a cloudy October sky before he bade farewell—a gentler one than Burton's—to the hotel pussycat, roses, and queerly croaking garden frogs and set off down the pass, alive that day with clouds of tiny sulphur-yellow butterflies drifting over the flowers, back to the almost forgotten prickly heat and perspiration of the plains.

I come across no artists today sitting before their easels squinting at a view of the formal patchwork, in every shade from terracotta to deep carmine, that the vegetable terraces snip out of the earth, mounted against the backing of the calm blue hills, or at a splendid torn flag of a sunset, or at a corner of some holy mound where the rocks have been devoutly daubed in brilliant wide stripes that resemble a football jersey. Some of the Governors' ladies, I believe, dabbled with a pretty brush and occasionally illustrated a volume of their jottings on happy days in the dear Nilgiris. Miss Dot Wapshare has a bundle of water-colour sketches that her rosy-cheeked grandfather (as he appears in a contemporary portrait) made of corners of Ooty, of his *syce* holding favourite ponies, and of the men in his regiment. But that was the period when it was perfectly usual for an officer to have a paintbox some-where in his kit and be able to dash off a pleasant little impression of a place for an album. Serious painters coming here, I think, might note a curious absence of mystery in the light, as though, perched on this lofty plateau, a mem-brane of atmosphere had been torn away between us and

113

the burning golden eye of the sun. Even at its loveliest, I feel, the landscape somewhere eludes the magic that would make artists long to paint it, and while it smiles in its disconcerting frankness, it seems to echo Lear's despairing dictum: 'Utterly undrawable.'

Yet it has never been the artists or the writers or the rich, after all, to whom Ooty has shown her fairest face— unless, that is, it happened that they delighted also in an outdoor life. If an occasional intellectual such as Sir C. P. Ramaswami Aiyar elects to settle here, protesting that it is the place that offers most out of all the world, its far more numerous and just as ardent devotees have always been the sportsmen and the naturalists, and not unusually someone who was both, such as Walter Campbell, the spirited young Highlander who described his ride up to Ooty in 1833 as passing out of the valley of death into Paradise. He kept a journal, too; it was published later in his life, long after he had left India, and his enthusiasm bubbles agreeably out of every page. When he came to Ooty, he was twenty years old, gay, sensible, compassionate, and in love with India, where he had been soldiering for three years. He was enjoying everything—shooting tiger; riding his little Arab mare, Turquoise, into a ballroom on a bet; learning from a couple of village poachers the technique of driving deer through the jungle by a clanging hand bell, with a brazier of live coals strapped to one man's head; reading natural history and making careful drawings of any rare animals he saw; tucking into his food 'like a ploughboy', as he says, and sleeping 'like a marine'. But this charming extrovert knew what he was talking about when he spoke of the valley of death. He had become hardened to seeing apparently healthy friends in his company struck down with black cholera and dying in a few hours. He had read the burial service himself over soldiers and their wives who were buried uncoffined in shallow graves hacked with pickaxes out of ground baked to rock, and his dwindling column had marched through a

114

land so smitten with famine that the silent villages they entered were strewn with corpses. Yet his natural flow of spirits was so unquenchable that he can relate with much amusement how, soon after the regiment took up its quarters in a terrible, pestilence-ridden fort, he was visited by a polite Eurasian gentleman who wished to sell him a highly desirable little plot in the new cemetery. He attributes the fact that he escaped where so many died to his practice of drinking medicinally a bottle of port a day.

Young Campbell came to Ooty twice, and his journal is ecstatic about the place. The furnished house that he shared with four friends who had come up with him for a shooting leave put him in mind not of a cow house but of 'a cottage *orné* on the banks of the Thames'. After breakfast, he walked out into the garden and snuffed the air scented with roses, heliotrope, mignonette, and violets. The rent of twenty-five pounds a month was a bit steep, perhaps, but he reflected that among five of them it did not work out too badly. He went out with a 'bobbery pack' of assorted tykes after sambar stag, noting disapprovingly that it was the Ooty sportsmen's habit to blaze away at hinds with calves as merrily as they did at stags, and he was intensely scornful of the ignorance of these poor Mulls (a disparaging nickname for the gentlemen of Madras, short for the mulligatawny soup featured so often on their menu), who talked about the wild animals by their wrong zoological names while barbarously decimating the population of the forests. And I read elsewhere that this steady, indiscriminate slaughter, in and out of season, by Mulls and others had indeed all but cleared the animals, big and small, out of the neighbourhood of Ooty by the seventies. The passing of the Nilgiri Fish and Game Act in 1878 saved them, and the Downs were finally made into one big wildlife reserve at the proposal of Lord Wenlock, the Governor of Madras after whom they are named.

Campbell preferred to go out stalking on the hills alone, as though he were home in the Highlands, in the intervals

115

of squiring little violet-eyed, dimpled Miss L——, who rode a brute of a pony like a pocket Fury and on whom he was, according to his cautious estimate, 'more than half spoony'. But there were so many things in Ooty that took up his thoughts. The puzzling native Todas and their marriage customs interested him greatly; he was charmed by the modest looks of the women. Though shooting was the real passion against which Miss L——'s dimples could not compete, he would pause in a day's sport to note an interesting bit of animal behaviour, or to wonder scientifically why and how the rare woodcock makes his long journey, unerring and punctual, to winter here in the remote Nilgiris, 'a mere mountain island surrounded by an ocean of burning plains', when there is 'no part of India nearer than the Himalayas where a woodcock could find rest for the sole of his foot'. He was a professional soldier with the curiosity of a born naturalist, and he might have ended contentedly settled in Ooty among all the other retired colonels (he became one), with his name on the gatepost of his own cottage *orné*, busily adding to the loaded shelves of works on Nilgiri wildlife in the library.

*

Even today, the wild is not as far away as you might suppose from all the tamed gardens and the peaceful bungalows. In Ooty's early days, it was nothing extraordinary for a nonplussed invalid taking the air to meet a great bull elephant ambling along the road doing the same thing and using half a tree as a fly whisk. A Victorian lady, peeping out of a bush where she and her servants had taken shelter, watched an elephant humourist twirling her vacated palanquin by one of its poles until it broke like an eggshell, then dancing on the wreck and capering off into the jungle with, she noted, a pleased horse laugh. Tigers were often seen in the station. There used to be a house, wistfully named Tudor Hall (it has long disappeared), that was more aptly rechristened Tiger Hall in 1855 after one

116

appeared in the compound, sat down like a big house cat, and benignly surveyed the settlement. I meet an old lady who remembers her husband's shooting a tiger on a domestic-looking little hill running up from the town, and can point to its huge, moth-eaten skin splayed out, the beautiful, undimmed savage head snarling towards the floor, on her sitting-room wall. But now the elephants stay down in the jungles below Ooty, and only the Todas, who live remote from other men among the spirit-haunted trees and rocks, may sometimes see a tiger. The dams being built out on the Downs, and the trucks rattling back and forth to the new factory, and the comings and goings of the forestry work gangs will surely drive the wild animals who lie up in the *sholas* farther away from Ooty.

All the same, there are occasional reminders that the animals are still here. Among the flowery cretonnes and the many photograph frames of a European sitting-room that might be in Tunbridge Wells, I hear one Ooty lady warning another to be careful about letting out the dogs for an evening run, since a hyena, who is apparently a well-known local character, is once more roaming the town. Pets disappear disconcertingly on walks now and then, I am told, and a panther killed a goat the other night in the neighbourhood of the golf course. And one morning in the Library I am introduced by Miss Myers to a fresh-faced Englishwoman, dressed in tweeds that match her blue eyes, with pearl drops bobbing from her ears, who unexpectedly says that she loves living in Ooty because here she can indulge her passionate interest in wild animals. She and her servant go down to the game reserves in Mysore State and stay for a week or so at a time to watch the bison, the different kinds of deer, the monkeys, and sometimes the panthers and elephants. One has to be a bit careful with elephants, says this placid lady, who looks, with her library books under her arm and her long earrings swinging, as though she had just stepped in from some strikingly unperilous village green.

As for domestic animals, the Dog is almost as strong in Ooty, I gather, as the Horse used to be in the halcyon days of the Ootacamund Club. The Savoy Hotel, which has one of the loveliest gardens in the place, takes (no doubt for that reason) a rare unfavourable stand against man's four-footed friends and has discreetly placed on the entrance veranda the most courteous of polished-brass plates, which seems to whisper its request, 'Please No Dogs.' But elsewhere they are greatly in evidence, as signs that a few British are still around in the flesh and very much in the spirit, I see a Labrador sitting, patient and dignified and clothed in eye-catching pastel fur, like royalty, in the back of an imported British sports car, and elderly dachshunds waddling along under the mimosas, and a brace of aged and staunchly quivering terriers held on leash by an equally antique-looking servitor while they wait for somebody outside Higginbotham's, and before whom a stout European lady in a khaki topee and a Fair Isle jumper crouches suddenly and emits crooning noises. There is a strong doggy set in Ooty; the Dog Show is a great event of the season. A retired Indian Army colonel breeds Alsatians, which are particularly popular here; other amateurs go in for Great Danes or wire-haired terriers.

Far outnumbering the aristocrats, of course, are the town's pi-dogs, who are rounded up now and then by the municipality in pogroms that quite often liquidate a few dogs with loving owners by mistake. I meet them all over the place, frisking through the bazaar and under the wheels of passing trucks in aimless community lechery that will populate the earth with more oversized tails and uncertainly flopping ears, or a solitary one cruising among the houses, turning its sharp nose hopefully towards a piece of blowing paper or a torn sack or anything that might contain a scrap of food. At night, I often hear a dog, or perhaps a couple of them, rummaging about on my veranda at Willingdon House; once, thoughts of the local hyena were re-edited by a shatteringly loud bark that

118

seemed to come from the wardrobe. It is on behalf of these unfortunates that the national characteristics of the remaining British residents flower as sturdily as ever. Nowhere is the flag shown more unmistakably than in the gently cranky (as other races are apt unsympathetically to regard it) fervour of the love affairs that some of them maintain with the animal kingdom. Scraggy dogs steer a course towards European back doors as unerringly as the woodcock makes his arrow flight to the Nilgiris. Sometimes the established dog of the house, having sized up his owners, brings along a hungry chum or two, who move in permanently forthwith. I hear of an ingenious resident who carefully piles an edifice of tins on her veranda before retiring, so that one of her *protégés*—a dog who for some reason finds it impossible to turn up until after dark—will knock it over and waken her to come down and give him a bowl of scraps. Lonely ladies who live valorously on incomes that one politely suspects are minuscule somehow contrive to save up little bags of food—like tender-hearted Miss Henrietta Noble in *Middlemarch* surreptitiously pocketing sugar lumps from the tea table for her poor children—which they carry on their walks to give to regular pensioners lying in wait for them by appointment. When I walk near the Club, I sometimes notice a thin cat lurking in the hedge, narrowly inspecting the parties of men and women going by on their way back to their villages from market, or the town bus snorting round a corner, a slender brown hand emerging from the driver's window to make some ineffably graceful wiggle of its fingers to a wildly honking car, or maybe an errand boy wrapped in dawdling appreciation of the melancholy warbling voice proceeding from the transistor strapped to his bicycle carrier. The spectator cat, I discover, is keeping his eyes skinned for his free meal ticket, who comes regularly for a walk along this road, and, sure enough, one day I see him stalk out to salaam the patroness, who nods pleasantly and opens her handbag.

119

Then, there are the protectors of sick ponies and cows, before whose well-known hospitable gates the bony veterans may appear as though by magic overnight, and the indomitable attackers of the owners of cruelly over-loaded bullock carts and of stout men piled up like white cotton bolsters in tiny, quaking pony gharries. The heart must have an outlet, but in Ooty the choice for Europeans, who seem mostly to have few family ties left, and those few many thousands of miles away, is more than usually meagre. The likeness to a restricted shipboard life, with its disciplines and substitutes, strikes one often; the death of one friend or the departure of another from the dwindling European passenger list leaves a sudden blank. There seems to be a queer sort of stoicism here, which maybe has picked up a bit of the Indian philosophy, too, to the solitary human condition. And perhaps that is why the affections appear so frequently to be concentrated on grateful, loving animals, whose places can, anyway, be filled when they vanish, or sometimes on wild creatures—animals or birds—who demand or give nothing and may be observed going about their strange lives in splendid indifference.

The dogged British right to be eccentric if one wishes seems to flourish in the rarefied air of the mountains, I think, and always has done so. There was a general's lady in Ooty in the seventies who lived in a house, now gone, called Bella Vista. At that time, there must have been a lot of talk about gold, for traces of it had been found in the quartz of the Nilgiri Hills. Mrs. General Thatcher had a dream revealing to her that there was a large deposit of gold in the grounds of Bella Vista. A forceful lady, she collected a gang of coolies next morning and started them digging, and she collared the officer commanding the engineers and requested him to let her have fifty men right away. When he declined, she managed to have some miners sent up from the plains; her talent for recounting dreams convincingly must have been remarkable. All they did

120

was to strike water and blow up an unlucky coolie. Mrs. Thatcher's folly ended as a pond. But the local people believed her dream. They say that gold *was* there, under the special protection of a powerful demon. The demon had caused the impious coolie to be blown to fragments. They understood and took pleasure in the British lady's fantasy, as Londoners wink solemnly at each other over some notably eccentric piece of behaviour. And even today there are Mrs. Thatchers around, and demons. I hear of a European resident whose illness cannot be diagnosed by the doctors at the hospital, and who is therefore positive in his own mind that the mysterious malady must be caused by a curse that some enemy has laid on him. And, walking about Ooty, I see solitaries whose fantasies are expressed in their air of existing sternly in another epoch, and even another world—old men on whose gaunt frames hang loose clothes of antique cut, and elderly women whose cheeks have an eternal peony bloom of youth in the glow of their daintily tilted parasols, and boldly individual dressers such as the lady who wears men's socks and garters and heavy brogues with her cotton frocks. Perhaps the most outstandingly English thing that was imported here when the hill station began was the national habit of preferring not to notice; the Indian shopkeepers and passersby regard their foreigners with deadpan tolerance as they go their ways. After all, they will not look upon anybody in the least like them again.

An acquaintance takes me, one perfect late afternoon, to call at a European home that I must not, she says, miss seeing, for it is itself a sort of dream. Earlier in the afternoon, in the garden of Willingdon House, the old *mahli*, who would be indistinguishable from the earth if it were not for the faded red turban rakishly twisted around his head, has been setting out little seedling annuals that mark, like green guiding traceries on a needlework canvas, where the bold summer blocks of pinks and oranges and blues will be stitched in. Then he sits on his heels patiently erecting palisades of thorny twigs to protect the seedlings from the predatory munchings of any passing cow. Now, while I stroll waiting for my friend, he is staggering back and forth with watering cans, quarrelling with the thin, dark girl who helps him fill them somewhere in the shade where the violets grow thickly. 'That reminds me, I must go round to the Botanical Gardens tomorrow and buy one or two boxes of anchusa for the Library garden,' says Miss Myers, stepping forth from her veranda as reliably as a wooden weather lady emerging from a weatherhouse, for it is Thursday, and the hour, right on the tick, when she goes for a walk that will finish at the Club for the usual bridge four. She swings up the drive to the road, and presently, my friend having arrived in her car, I follow her.

There is no faded red turban bobbing busily about in the compound of this house I am being taken to visit, and I think it must be many years since there was one. When we turn in at the gates, the car grumbles along spasmodically through potholes. The garden has almost elected to return to the wild hills. Here and there, the shape of formal flower beds can be made out through choking grass, and enormous flowering shrubs are engaged in eating each other, a feast at once cannibal and vegetarian; a vast, knotted wisteria with frightening biceps has slipped a thuggee's scarf round the veranda and is getting down to garrotting the house. Our hostess, a frail elderly figure in a little grey knitted cardigan, comes to meet us and complains, shaking her head at the matted garden, that people from the town come up and steal her shrubs. She is the widow of a prosperous local businessman, who brought her to this house as a bride sixty years ago; she mentions later that she still has her wedding dress put away somewhere. She and her daughter live quite alone in this sizeable house, without a single servant, by what I feel must be sturdily quixotic choice; I have been told that she owns a good slice of the very choicest property in Ooty.

We pass through a perfect zoo of game heads mouldering on the lofty walls of a dark hall, daring you, in their awful, ultimate deadness, to believe that they could ever have skipped upon the Downs or leaped through the hot, scrubby jungle. The large, cold room in which we are asked to sit down is so full of things that I hardly know where to look first. There are, lined against the walls like dishevelled dowagers at a ball, threadbare Victorian chairs that have burst their buttons and sometimes plead a hernia of the springs as well, and edifices of bamboo or japanned wood loaded with a multitude of small china and glass knick-knacks, and innumerable yellow photographs of floating-ectoplasm faces, and loyal pictures of British royalty. An ancient horn gramophone rears up to the high roof, like some marine monster in the aquarium light, beside a dusty stack of records. 'The gramophone is hers,' says our hostess indulgently, looking at her middle-aged daughter. She speaks of the 'dame's school', long disappeared, where she used to go, for she was brought up in Ootacamund, and she remembers the early part of the century when visitors came up from the plains by tonga, a sort of low gig drawn by two horses that would have to be changed two or three times on the way. All her old friends have gone now, she says, and though one feels that she probably keeps a sharp business eye on the town from her extraordinary watchtower and is alive to every change in it, she goes out seldom; her daughter does the shopping in the market and looks after their affairs. The house has a mildewed smell of India, but it is also pure Perrault—a place over which a spell must have been cast, where the weeds have grown, the clocks have stopped, and one would not be surprised to step over a sleeping scullion or two.

Many old houses in Ooty are sad, and some of them, like this one, are eerie. Sir Frederick Price, the hill station's loving historian, declares that in spite of the various persistent stories of hauntings 'there is not a single self-respecting ghost in Ooty'. But I am informed just as firmly that this is not so by a lively and attractive grey-haired woman who insists that Ooty is full of ghosts, including the shade of a horticulturist who turns up from time to time in her own garden. Mrs. Carter is one of the few European residents I meet who runs a business—making and marketing farmhouse cheeses. Having noted that fresh cheese is a rare delicacy in India and that Ooty's pastures provide much milk, she learned the art from a farmer in Devon when she was on a trip to England some years ago. Business has been thriving, and she has customers all over India. Mrs. Carter does the cheese-making herself, with the aid of one boy she trained to help her, in the cottage where she and her husband, a retired tea planter from Ceylon, live with an assortment of dogs. They love Ooty and plan to end their days here. Mr. Carter is a pillar of St. Stephen's Church, and also interests himself in the Library and other local affairs. The small garden of their cottage is stuffed with all sorts of flowers growing together in tolerance and the wrong seasons—English violets lying down with the canna, hyacinths from Kashmir blooming at the same time as the China roses and larkspur and lilies, and mimosa, with its expensive South of France air, floating, a pale-sulphur cloud in the air, next to a tree hung with the great tropical white-mutton-fat bells of the datura. It does not surprise me to learn that Mrs. Carter's ghost is a gardener, too—an old English lady, she says briskly, who used to live in the cottage and is now and then seen by the servants as well, an unalarming phantom pottering approvingly among the flowers.

PART SEVEN

CHURCH bells always seem to be ringing somewhere in Ooty. Because St. Stephen's, the Protestant church, is close to Willingdon House, I hear its unmistakably British voice loudest on a Sunday morning, but I know that bells are also ringing from mission chapels and the big Catholic church farther off, and from the Nazareth Convent, founded ninety-one years ago, where the sisters in their white cashmere habits teach a hundred and twenty girls, of whom only nine are Catholic and the rest are of the Hindu or Parsi faiths. And to the Christian pealings is added one Sunday a merry little kick of drums from down in the town, for it is Pongal, the winter-solstice festival celebrating the arrival of spring and the blossoms. Festivals of one kind or another come thick and fast here, and the telegraph office lists cheap-rate standard messages by which you may wish your friends 'Warmest Holi Greetings' or 'Warmest Pongal Greetings' or whatever suits the occasion. On the Library noticeboard I have studied the list of public holidays, on some of which the Reading Room may remain open to members—two days of Pongal, the end of the Mohammedan feast of Ramadan, and Republic Day, all in January; Telugo New Year, in March; then Good Friday and Independence Day; Sri Jayamti, in September, and Aynda Pooja, in October; and so on through the spiritual and temporal calendar devised for the mutual refreshment of gods and men. There is something for everybody up here. After a bit, Christ and Krishna and Mohammed are apt to

127

run together at the edges and seem indistinguishable; the roof of brilliant blue sky, appearing to be so near and beaming impartially, houses all quite comfortably.

Today, when I have decided to go to church, the drums tap briskly away, celebrating the imminent opening of the wild flowers on the hills, which I cannot stay to see, and the arrival soon of all the best summer birds, who dart up to Ooty like snobbish visitors for the season. The over two hundred varieties of flowers noted by the French naturalist who accompanied Mr. Sullivan into the hills in 1819 are more than doubled by Professor P. F. Fyson, of Presidency College, Madras, and Lady Bourne in their 'Flora of the Nilgiri Hill-Tops', published in 1915, and they list very many English names—buttercups, harebells, anemones, dog roses, wild orchids, strawberry flowers, the downy clematis called Traveller's Joy, the tiny aromatic pink Herb Robert, and the pimpernel that opens and shuts its bloodshot eye to the sun. If I were staying in Ooty longer, I might see them, and also the arrival of such delightful-sounding birds as the blue-necked bee-eater and the Indian plaintive cuckoo and the emerald cuckoo, and whole families of woodpeckers, owls, and nightjars. I wish that I could catch a glimpse, perhaps, of the Deccan scimitar babbler, of whom the charming writer on Indian birds Sálim Ali says, 'The birds are as a rule shy and quiet skulkers, but will sometimes boldly enter town limits in quiet hill stations.' At the moment, I must admit, the overpowering note of the dawn chorus is gratingly supplied by a non-skulker who is neither shy nor quiet—the common Indian crow. 'His intelligence and boldness,' says Sàlim Ali sternly, 'coupled with an infinite capacity for scenting and avoiding danger, carry him triumphantly through a life of sin and wrong-doing.' Black as jet, brilliant as diamonds, this bad subject often leans towards me by day from a low branch of one of the trees up the hotel drive, wickedly eyeing my head as though debating whether to sharpen his own formidable ebony scimitar on it. But if his voice is clamorous in argument from dawn to dusk, I enjoy listening to a pair of bulbuls, the birds from a Persian poem, who disconcertingly remind me of English thrushes as they practise their sweet notes to one another in the acacias. Altogether English, a slender grey wagtail exclaims 'Chiswick! Chiswick!' as he runs across the lawn flirting his tail, and tries continually to get into Miss Myers' bathroom. This morning he is joined by a hoopoe, splendid in his crested turban and pale tan-and-white striped coat, who inserts his long, reedy beak into the turf and keeps it there pensively for a moment or so, like a doctor popping in a thermometer, before taking it out and flying off to test the next lawn.

The drums, ushering in the new term of lovely summer, have stopped suddenly, and St. Stephen's bell tower, wheezily clearing its throat, begins to sing in a thin, elderly voice three verses of 'O God our help in ages past', with one note flat. One finds oneself waiting for the bell to crack, while reflecting that it is wonderful, really, how the old things manages to do it at all. Somehow, the British Sunday has been left behind here as a legacy. I notice a sort of Sabbatical flatness and deadness in the street as I walk towards St. Stephen's. The church is approached uphill between splendid trees; built in 1830, it was perhaps dedicated, as a graceful compliment, to the name saint of the Right Honourable Stephen Lushington, Governor of Madras at the time, who laid its foundation stone. It is a stone building in the Gothic style, the colour of clotted Cornish cream, with a sturdy tower and pinnacles and a wide, airy porch. One can imagine it being spirited away entire and set down without jarring the landscape among pollarded elms in Surrey or Hampshire, until one notices that this is skilfully Indianized Gothic; the porch with its high, flat front and flattened arch might equally well lead into a mosque, and it marries better to eucalyptus and cypress than to elms. In Ooty, many things come under the same umbrella without difficulty.

But when I go inside, arriving somewhat out of breath just as St. Stephen's frail soprano bell jerks out 'To endless years the same' and abruptly falls silent, like a run-down holy musical box, I enter an interior that must rejoice an exiled Anglican heart with the smell of hassocks and scrubbed wood, and the shine of brass, and the cheerful primary colours and well-fed-looking Biblical characters of Victorian stained glass. The roof is supported by glossy white-painted wooden columns that are savage exiles themselves in this calm setting, for I remember reading in the guidebook I bought at Higginbotham's that they are made of teak and were taken from the sacked palace of Tippu Sultan at Seringapatam after his final defeat by the British. On the walls of the porch and in the body of the church are many stone and brass tablets to the Indian civil servants, the magistrates, the soldiers, and the engineers who helped to build Ootacamund in her early days, or came here, loved her, and stayed for life. I notice a tablet to Helen Cecilia, the wife of John Sullivan, Ooty's original begetter, and to two of their children. And poor Lady Rumbold, whose husband built the mansion that became the Ootacamund Club, and who died in childbed, like so many of the Victorian wives in India, also rests somewhere here, among the memorials to the young soldiers and the administrators, and to the planters of South India who went from the Nilgiris to fight in the 1914 war. There is one to Colonel John Ochtherlony, a kinsman of the Misses Wapshare of Rosemount, who expired of jungle fever in 1863.

In the church, the past jostles and rubs elbows more vigorously than the present, which is already settled in the cane-seated pews, waiting for matins to begin. Its look is rather sparse. I imagine that on a Sunday before the war the pews would have been packed, and the cars would have been parked thickly up the drive, but only twenty of us, by my count, have responded this morning to St. Stephen's gallant little solo—fifteen Indians and five Europeans.

THE NILGIRI LIBRARY

VICTORIAN PILLAR-BOX, OOTY

THE CLUB, 1966

Photo: The Author

THE GRAVEYARD AT ST. STEPHEN'S

Photo: The Author

The children in the Indian family parties are smartly brushed and ribboned; the little girls' pigtails stand out wirily under the popular broad, flat bandeaux of massed pink and orange petals that I like to watch the flowerstall boys threading nimbly in the market. The Europeans, considerably more sombre in attire and older in years, include my acquaintance Mr. Carter, the retired tea planter, sitting in a front pew. We all clatter to our feet as the small choir enters, shepherded by a surpliced Indian who radiates good will from a face like a rising sun and is, someone tells me later, a lay preacher officiating in place of the rector, who is away on a visit. He begins the service, and the little organ, speaking up suddenly like the masculine half of the bell tower's ladylike voice, groans out the psalm. The singing rises thinly but valiantly to Tippu Sultan's roof beams. Presently, Mr. Carter goes up to the reading desk to give the lesson of the day. Very trim in his dark suit, he walks slowly, because of his arthritis, and hooks his sticks over the desk, but the English language treads firmly and nobly. We sit listening—a small party who would not fill up a lifeboat, beached in this Victorian ark that has come to rest seven thousand-odd feet up in the Nilgiris, on the toe of India. The little boys and girls fidget and drop their collection money. The European ladies' hats, which would translate perfectly to Surrey even if the church would not, do not quiver. The preacher gives his sermon and announces a hymn: 'We love the place, O God.' I have to note that this refers to the Church, and not, as for one absent-minded moment I thought it did, to Ooty, from which, seated as I am near the door, I fancy I can hear the distant pulsing of those festive drums floating in out of the sunshine.

After a sad-eyed Indian man in my pew has taken round the plate with an air of expecting no great surprise from its contents, and after our preacher has beamingly shaken our hands at the door, the congregation departs, in cars or on foot, down the hill. But I leave the church and turn the corner into the graveyard, where the dead crowd closer and whisper more intimately than they do in the St. Stephen's memorials, which are worldly, like a ledger totting up the price and losses and rewards of building an empire. This is the old British cemetery that Richard Burton said was already 'so extensive, so well stocked' when he came to Ooty in 1847 that it made him 'shudder to look at it', and it must have grown for many years after that. There is no room in it any longer; Anglican funerals today are held at the Church of St. Thomas, on the other side of Ooty.

The great trees that grow here trail their low, sweeping skirts of leaves across views of Ooty that must have been wide from this hill when they were first planted. I get glimpses of the red roofs and the blue hills between the branches, and I hear voices from the parties of townsfolk who are toiling up a path, cut in broad earth steps, that runs alongside the church, past a tiny wayside Hindu shrine, where a lamp always flickers, I know, among strewn marigold petals, and I can hear, too, the chatter of some women in faded blue-green saris who are scratching away with their mattocks at a vegetable terrace on a neighbouring hillside. But the voices and the faint hootings, barkings, tinklings, and murmurings that are the distant blended sounds of Ooty are far away and pure, as though coming across water. There is nobody in this green silence but a pi-dog slowly, thoughtfully sniffing in the grass; he trots away and jumps over a wall out of sight. The inmates of the place no longer have friends to visit them. I walk for a while among the vast nineteenth-century tombs, shaped like huge travelling trunks with domed lids, which would be unpacked, their occupants surely felt, at the Resurrection. There are some, of a pattern that I do not remember seeing before, like low Roman couches, or even sideboards, supported by massive lion's-paw feet. One, enclosed in a neat cubicle of iron railings, is a tidy little bed with a smooth marble bolster

132

at its head. The British who were left behind in Ooty were to be furnished as domestically and handsomely as possible.

Even in this tonic air, I note, the expectation of life in the early days seems to have been low. Twenty to thirty-five is a big age group among these officers of the Bengal Native Infantry, the Bombay Cavalry, the Dragoons who lie here, sometimes with their wives and children, lined up so thickly that the paths seem like the aisles between closely packed hospital cots. The implacable British snobbery, operating in death as in life, divides off the different social stations into cubicles of more than iron. I do not come across any enlisted men here; I fancy that they are buried in the old military cemetery down in Wellington. But the children would almost occupy a hospital to themselves; the graveyard adds to St. Stephen's recording ledger a fearsome statement on the Victorian mortality rate, heightened by India. Here are the countless infant sons who came to nothing, treading on each other's heels, and the pale garlands of infant daughters—the Sophias and Amys, the Johns and Walters. The shorter their lives, it often seems, the more tremendous the edifices erected over them by their sorrowing parents, as though to make up with masonry for the length of time that they ought to have occupied on the face of the earth. Sometimes the actual span is recorded with touching fidelity: 'James beloved son, departed this life October 1855 aged seven years, seven months, and twenty days.' I observe the tomb of the Honourable Henry Handcock, A.D.C. to His Excellency Lord Harris, Governor of Madras; he was killed by a tiger, it says, on December 16, 1858. And here, too, are the settlement's first chaplain, and members of the family of the Mr. McIvor, who was sent for from Kew to plant the Botanical Gardens, and scores of British men and women of whom nothing is recorded except that they came to India and Ooty and, for one reason or another, laid their bones in the place.

Looking at the solid shape of Mr. Lushington's church

over all the quiet company, I think of the sententious words written by a Captain Limond in 1832 in praise of the Governor's enthusiastic interest in the building of Ootacamund. 'It will be the glory of Mr. Lushington's Government, without extravagant hyperbole, that he introduced Europe into Asia in the Nilgiris' was the Captain's confident assertion. 'In the process of time they will become one of the noblest colonies in the known world.' And John Sullivan prophesied, as Sir Frederick Price has written, that Ooty would become an England in the tropics, 'a land where the European would increase and multiply, raise all manner of farm, dairy, and garden produce, and make much money therefrom—in fact, an Indian Utopia'. It has not happened quite like that, though Ooty may still be an Indian Utopia. This select spot by the church, tented by lush trees, with an air at once romantic and passionately private that is characteristic of its inhabitants, is not a bad place for thinking about the processes of time and the fate of even the most solidly established glory. India and England meet along its paths. Here and there, a railing has broken, a few toes of a supporting lion's paw have chipped off one of the Roman couches and make it look as authentically antique as any crumbling relic of empire found in a desert. All sorts of small ferns and wild flowers, yellow and white, grow in the rough grass and have seeded with Indian largesse in the cracks in the masonry, stretching hairy little green arms over the tablets as though to obliterate all traces. India is really winning. And, walking round, reading the names and breathing the warm Nilgiris smell of cypress and eucalyptus, I find it easy to understand the European residents who say they will never leave now, though so many of their community have gone and the ranks grow thinner, for Ooty is home.